Hunting Western Deer

A Complete Guide to Deer Hunting

By Jim & Wes Brown

PUBLISHED BY:

JIM, CHRIS & WES BROWN

COPYRIGHT © 1991

LIBRARY OF CONGRESS
CATALOGING IN PUBLICATION

CATALOG NO. 452011

I.S.B.N. 0-912299-51-7

TITLE: *HUNTING WESTERN DEER*

Jim, Chris & Wes Brown
P.O. Box 634
Boring, Oregon 97009

CREDITS

Oregon Department of Fish and Wildlife (Biology Reports and Statistics)

Our Family, Friends and Hunting Partners (Theories and General Information)

Wes Brown, Jim Brown, Christina Brown, Ray Brown, and our Hunting Party (Research and Organization)

Our Family (Cooking Recipes)

Christina Brown, Virginia Brown (Proofreading and Editing)

Cover photo by Calie Yoder

TABLE OF CONTENTS

INTRODUCTION

Do you enjoy deer hunting? This book is designed for the beginner as well as the experienced deer hunter. This is not your run-of-the-mill, "how-to" deer hunting book. The material gathered in this book leads you to the question of "how come?" A few examples are: How come 80% of the deer harvested each year are harvested by 20% of the same hunters? And, how come 20% of the harvested deer are harvested by 80% of the remaining hunters? You might know a hunter, maybe someone at work or a friend, who gets his or her deer every year. "How come?" It might be because they go the extra mile it takes for today's hunter to be successful. Maybe they have realized that knowledge is the key to being a successful hunter.

Our book looks at the pros and cons to all phases of deer hunting from preparation, scouting techniques, to hunting strategies, meat care, home butchering, and finally, antler mounting. Whether you hunt with bow or gun, for mule deer or blacktail deer, from tree stands or stalking in roaded areas or wilderness, this book will make a difference in the coming years.

The statistics we have in this book will enlighten you to theories and conjecture that is food for thought. Looking at this information you will begin to ask questions about your past hunting trips. Hopefully, you will begin to see whether you did or did not make mistakes.

You probably will not agree with everything in this book, but it will be interesting to see what conclusions you draw from reading *HUNTING WESTERN DEER*.

CHAPTER 1

PICKING YOUR HUNTING PARTNER

A. WHAT IS A TYPE "A" HUNTER

At some point you will realize hunting partners determine the success or failure of your trip. The Type "A" hunter is the kind of hunter who will drive all night to get to his destination, then be ready to hunt at daylight. Hunting down to the very bottom of the canyons and up to the highest mountain ridge, the Type "A" hunter is dedicated. Some say he is obsessed; we say he knows what he wants out of the hunt and accomplishes it. Obsession makes him the hunter he is — usually the best in the party. Type "A's" are very knowledgeable hunters. They read abundantly about hunting and draw their own conclusions, regardless of popular opinion. These hunters could be your best and most knowledgeable hunting source.

Being punctual is an endearing quality of a Type "A" hunter. Looking for someone who did not show up and then finding out he never left camp will make any hunter angry as he wasted good hunting time waiting for the "lost" hunter.

Type "A's" observe new techniques that may not be proven as yet but show promise for his type of hunting. Most

"A's" have some trophies from previous hunts. This is evident by the antlers and heads in their dens at home. We do think there are more Type "A" men hunters than Type "A" women hunters but the Type "A" women hunters you do find are excellent hunters.

We are aware of the Type "A's" and the Type "B's" in our party. You should make a list of all your hunting partners, look at each person and place them in the A or B category. Remember there is nothing wrong with being in either slot. Each has advantages and disadvantages.

Type "A's" and "B's" camp together well but they should not hunt together. Try to pick the same type hunter as you are to hunt with. My son and I hunt well together. You can see in picture 1-A my son Westley and his first buck taken with a bow.

If you are a Type "A" hunter and try to hunt with a Type "B" hunter, he will try to talk you out of going into the deep canyons, hunting rugged hilltops, etc. This constant conflict of interest can make the Type "A" hunter very frustrated as it diminishes his hunt.

Type "A's", I am sure, do not enjoy camp as much as Type "B's" do. But "A's" do not care for camping as much as hunting. Type "A's" prefer checking hunting logs to help them decide where and when to hunt. Comparing antlers as they hunt, they will try to harvest the best trophy. Two typical Type "A" hunters are my son and I shown in picture 1-B.

B. WHAT IS A TYPE "B" HUNTER

By comparing the Type "B" hunter with the Type "A" hunter, you will find the two types have many differences. The "B's" lack the immense hunting desire the Type "A's" have. For example, if Type "B's" are extremely tired at 2 a.m. they will roll over and sleep in. The "B's" are most likely to get up late and be late for departure time. They enjoy the trip more than the hunt. Another trait "B's" have is they don't think about hunting until it is almost time for the hunt and are more likely not to get a deer every year.

Comforts of home while on the hunting trip are important to "B's". They like to make things as cheerful as possible while they are there. We enjoy spending time with "B's" in camp as we can let off some steam while on a long week's hunt.

A "B" hunter will look for the best buys and compromise between price and quality. The "B" hunter will be distracted more than the Type "A". If he finds fishing more productive he will be reluctant to go back hunting. They are usually happy-go-lucky people. More women hunters are Type "B's" than men. We believe most women go hunting with their husbands to stay in camp than go to hunt. These conclusions are strictly from our years of hunting experience.

C. HOW LARGE MAY YOUR PARTY BE

Your hunting party may be as large as 20 people or as small as two people (one should avoid hunting alone). Looking

Photo 1B

at the pros and cons of each size, you can determine what size party you prefer to hunt with. In a large party you will have plenty of people to make large drives for deer, help with chores and have plenty of "B.S." It is true that a large party can share the expenses for the trip much easier than a smaller party but you also have more problems with sleeping arrangements and space for everyone to eat and stay dry and cool when the weather warrants it.

With a large party you have much more input on what the deer are doing, allowing you to make better decisions about hunting. On your drives you can cover all the escape routes the

Photo 1A

deer will use and more than one drive can be put on at the same time.

Also, with more people, you can always have someone going to town each day to bring in fresh supplies unless, of course, you are in an area where this is not possible.

On the other hand, small parties also have advantages and disadvantages. First, you have less equipment to carry into camp and you can hunt smaller areas. Most of the time you can camp closer to your hunting area because fewer people make less noise and the quality of companionship is sometimes better. Some disadvantages are that you may be shorthanded for getting your deer skinned and meat cared for and everyone will have to participate in your drives. Try to get into town every three days to alleviate boredom. Each time you go to town you should go with a different person. Allowing time away from each other will help tension to dissipate. Everyone should have the opportunity for time by themselves.

D. WHAT IS A "STUMBLE-BUM HUNTER"

We need to inform you about another type of hunter we call the "Stumble-Bum Hunter." Do not let the name fool you. They are usually fair hunters — but they lack the knowledge to be great hunters. You will know these kinds of hunters by their actions. They purchase their licenses on the last day before the season begins. Usually they have done little or no scouting or preparation of any kind. If you look at their success ratios, they are very unsuccessful. However, they do get a deer once in a while. This is due to complete luck rather than any skill. Their equipment is usually mismatched and disorganized. We feel many hunters fall into this category. However, with the right guidance, knowledge and a little common sense they could become more successful.

For just a moment we need to mention a sore subject — the "Slob Hunter" — one who violates the hunting codes of others, laws, etc. They are very few in number but they give all hunters a bad name. All too often good hunters lose face in the general public's eye because of this minority of slob hunters. By the way, if you know a "Slob Hunter" — avoid him as he can and will hinder you in your hunting endeavors.

Hundreds of people have been injured in years past from "intoxicated hunters." There is no need for this as alcohol should be used sparingly or not at all. You should be capable of making rational decisions for the safety of you and others around you.

E. KNOWLEDGE IS THE KEY TO SUCCESS

Most hunters think they know all there is about deer hunting but as knowledge is gained everyone should and will learn new methods and skills, which definitely will put you on your way to becoming a continuously successful deer hunter.

After reading this book and applying our techniques, you will sight more deer, have more shots and, hopefully, harvest more deer.

CHAPTER 2

ORGANIZING YOUR HUNTING PARTY

A. DESIGNATING A HUNTMASTER

What is a huntmaster you ask? He is the one who organizes hunting affairs for the year. It is a very strenuous job as you will learn. Try not to burden the same person with this duty year after year.

The huntmaster plans camp preparations, beginning with supplies such as rolls of plastic, staples, staple gun, hammer and nails and other gear. He also plans camp assembly, prepares a list showing all the duties that have to be performed. Aside from all this, he has the duty to determine how much each person is going to pack.

Before making a backpacking trip, you need to do physical conditioning. You don't have to be an Arnold Schwarzennegger to backpack, but you should be able to walk up and down hills without much effort. Wheezing, coughing and such can alarm deer of your presence. Consult your physician and set up your own program to meet your needs.

The formula we use to determine each person's pack weight capabilities is to begin with their height. An example of this formula: I am 6 feet tall (round to next half number such as 5.5 for 5'5" tall or 5 for 5'2" tall); add two, making 8; then add a 0 to the end of the number and I should pack 80 lbs. (5.5, add 2 is 7.5, attach 0 is 70 1/2 pounds.) Now determine how much you are overweight from the doctor's chart. (If you get a negative number you should not be packing.) I am overweight 40 lbs. So we deduct 1/2 of 40 lbs. which is 20 lbs. from the 80 lbs. leaving 60 lbs. The last step — and you must be honest with this one — is, "What kind of shape am I in?" If you are in excellent shape you would carry 60 lbs. But, if you are in good shape, deduct five pounds from the total, leaving 55 pounds. Or, if you determine you are in only fair shape, deduct another 5 pounds, leaving 50 pounds. In my case I have a bad back from the heavy work I have done, so I would carry no more than 50 pounds. But let us say you have a different problem such as a leg problem or minor medical problems, etc. You then should carry 5 to 10 lbs. less, making your total 45 or 40 pounds. Using this formula will allow your huntmaster to put together customized loads for each person.

Remember the number of trips you will have to make depends on how many people you have and how much gear you have to move. This has been the best way we have used to determine pack weight. It is better to make a few more trips, though, rather than injure yourself trying to carry too much.

No matter how much you carry or what your physical condition is under any load, try to walk slower than you would normally walk and rest often enough so as not to create any other serious physical problem. Resting places should be marked along the trail and you should have a supply of water. Most people walk about 1 1/2 miles an hour with a pack on. Also, remember that without a load, you cover the same amount of distance in about half the time. You have to allow for unloading and reloading time at the end of each trip. Normally this takes about 30 minutes.

If you are shorthanded on packers you can do what we call leap-frog your packs in. To do this, take one pack in one-fourth the total distance and stash it. Return for your second pack, take it in beyond the first pack to the halfway point of camp. Hide it and return to the first pack. Carry the first pack three-fourths of the way to camp and so on until you have both packs in camp. Some people, after taking their first load to camp will remain to begin arranging and assembling camp while the other members of the party, who we call "mules", will continue to carry the remaining loads for the day.

In order to operate your camp smoothly, beginning from the first day, you must arrange three areas first — the kitchen, potty room, and sleeping quarters. On the second day some people continue to pack gear while others start the process of wood cutting and arranging the rest of camp.

The huntmaster should set up a file system at home to keep all hunting and scouting logs on file. If you fill out a log each day and turn it in, you will have a running account of your scouting and hunting days. Along with this, the huntmaster has the responsibility of keeping the handmade map up-to-date. Usually this is kept hanging in a central gathering location such as the eating area. We will discuss handmade maps in another chapter.

B. CROSS COUNTRY TRAVELING

As you will be going off in the woods often, knowledge of cross-country traveling is important. Even in roaded areas this can be a problem. Seventy-five percent of all people who hunt are reluctant to venture off the roads for fear of getting lost.

You may find informative books on this subject in the library. However, we will give you some basic pointers regarding equipment you may need. To begin your journey cross country, the first item to purchase is a good compass. Plan on spending around ten dollars or more. Remember, a compass is no good without a map of the area and the knowledge of how to use it. Most books inform you in determining true North from magnetic north. Practice using the compass and map many times before you go.

Before attempting cross-country travel, purchase a good

topographical map of your hunting area. This will give you more knowledge of the basic terrain. After obtaining your maps, look at the key to see what all the symbols mean. Keeping your maps in a sealed plastic bag, such as a Ziploc, will prevent moisture from ruining them. Be sure to note the distance of scale for your map. You need this information to insure the places you will be searching have the correct combination of deer habitat.

C. ROADED AREA HUNTING

The major differences between hunting deer in roaded areas and wilderness areas are that roaded areas allow you to cover more terrain and they usually provide easier going. You get lost much less, you can return more often to camp, and it is easier scouting during preseason sessions. This method may be easier to spot deer movement but the deer will be more alert for danger. If you are installing tree stands, roaded areas make it easier to carry your saw, hammer and nails, etc. Carrying a plywood stand and all the other items you will need can be very laborious if you have to haul them for any great distance.

You can move much more quietly hunting roaded areas, provided you are on a dirt road. Gravel roads are very noisy to walk on and will alarm deer of your presence. Deer are more wary on roaded areas because of the constant traffic. Deer will hear vehicles coming about 50 yards away as they have about ten times better hearing than we do. Deer tend to cross roads quickly and if you see one you will usually get running sightings at best. As in Figure 2-A, you can see a forky crossing the road on a dead run. When walking the roads, you can expect deer to be standing alongside the road or maybe even in the middle of the road if you are lucky. As an experiment, try standing off a well-used road, watching vehicles go by. A small distance off the road you will see that people riding in a vehicle will not see you. You will hear the vehicles coming sooner than you will see them. The deer do the same thing and have better hearing than you do. On gravel the noise is even more noticeable. As you pass deer, you

Photo 2A

reinforce this danger signal that is along the roads. When hunting these areas, you are hunting disturbed deer which is twice as difficult as hunting undisturbed deer. If you have ever shut a car door and heard the noise it makes, you will know that there is no other sound in nature that sounds like that. All deer are aware of at that point is danger coming from that direction.

D. WILDERNESS AREA HUNTING

There is a great advantage to hunting wilderness areas. First, you have at least one-tenth the amount of people hunting these areas. Most people are not capable of these kinds of hunts. Hunting pressure on the deer in these areas is far less and hunting undisturbed deer is much easier. As hunting pressure is increased around the roaded areas, the deer will tend to move into the wilderness to escape that pressure. The conclusion we have drawn from our observations is that most trophy deer live in and around wilderness areas, which is why it is traditionally better hunting. It is also enjoyable to be in a place that is unspoiled by too many people. Be sure to leave your campsite as you found it, free of litter and as if no one had been there. Also, be sure to check with the Forest Service regarding the rules of your particular wilderness area.

Most deer living in the wilderness are in better shape than the deer in roaded areas. More preparation is required to hunt these places, but most of the time it will be worth the effort. As there are more and more hunters and less land open to the public each year, these prime hunting locations are getting to be more popular. If you have small children that show enthusiasm for hunting, you should begin scouting primitive spots for future hunts. To our knowledge, none of the wilderness areas have ever been changed to an access area.

To acquire maps of these areas you can contact the Department of Fish and Wildlife, P.O. Box 3503, Portland, Oregon 97208 or Region 6 of the National Forest Service, 319 S.W. Pine St., Box 3623, Portland, Oregon 97208. Be sure you have a good idea of the map you want as there are many to choose from. The cost for each map is between $3.00 and $5.00.

Horse packing is a good way to hunt back country, but keeping a horse for use once a year is very expensive. In talking to horse packers, a riding horse is worth between $300.00 and $500.00. But a packhorse that will pack goods and dead animals, which is unnatural to a horse, is worth $600.00 to $800.00. As you can see, the cost factor eliminates this type of hunting for many people.

As you look at the entrances to some hunting areas, some are marked on the trailhead with a motorcycle with a circle and a line through it, followed by a horse with the same marks. These symbols designate this area as a foot traffic only area. It may state at the bottom of the sign, "foot traffic only." These types of areas are usually fairly small but worth the time spent to find them. Figure 2-B shows a nice four-point photographed in a wilderness area.

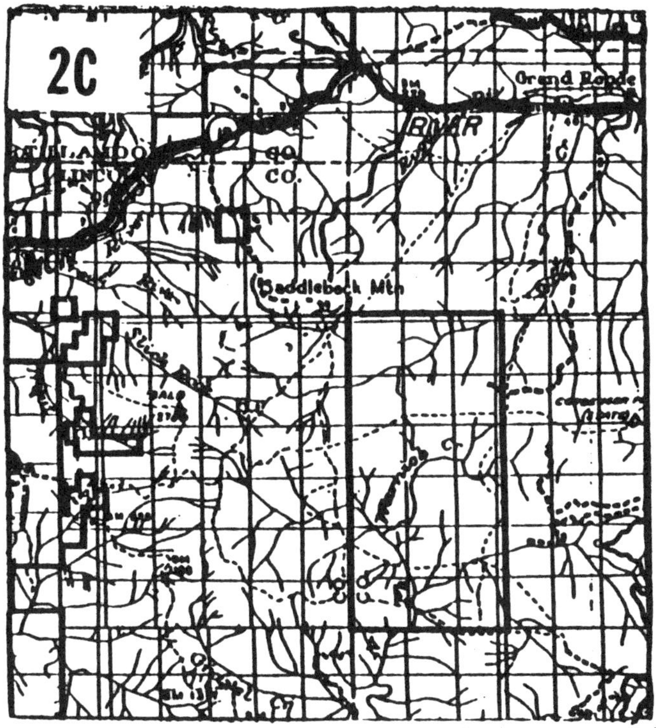
2C
Grand Ronde
RIVER
CO.
Saddleback Mtn

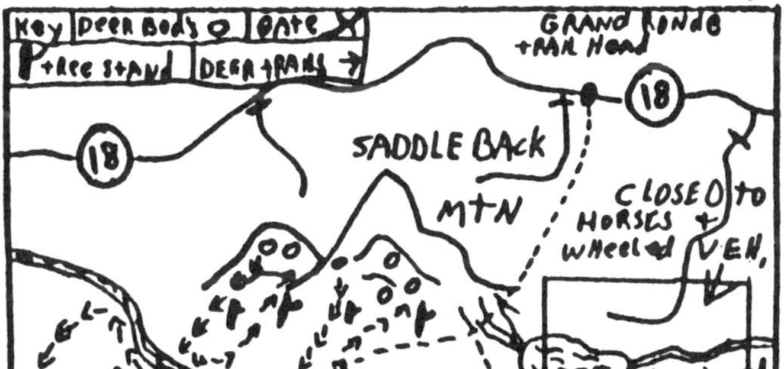
Key
Deer Beds
Gate
Tree stand
Deer trails
GRAND RONDE
TRAIL HEAD
18
18
SADDLE BACK
MTN
CLOSED TO
HORSES +
WHEELED VEH.
BIG TREE
WARNICK
CAMP
GRAVEL
CR.

Photo 2B

E. WILDERNESS SURVIVAL/EDIBLE PLANTS

One of the biggest fears that people have about wilderness travel is the fear of getting lost and starving or getting hurt and not being found. We will start with some facts about humans. For instance, how long do you think you can you live without food? It is about 30-35 days. This is not your primary problem however. The utmost basic necessity is heat and shelter. You can only live 24 hours without heat in moderate clothing in temperatures below 40 degrees, and a shorter time if it is colder. (This is not carved in stone for each person.) Forethought is the answer to this problem.

Water, however, is the most basic need for survival. The average person can live approximately six days without water. As you can see, food is your last priority. After your shelter is constructed and the fire is established, locating water and boiling for 10 minutes or using a water purifying pill is recommended. We prefer to boil the water 20 minutes for large amounts of water and use the pill also.

Your last necessity is to forage for food. You will find there is more value in roots than in greens. Clover plants may be eaten raw. Dandelion leaves may be made into a salad by adding a small amount of water. Do not eat any mushrooms as most of them are poisonous. Do not eat any plants with a milky sap.

You can make hot tea by chopping pine, fir, and spruce needles and boiling them in purified water for five minutes. It will help prevent scurvy and make you feel warmer. Fish, meat, greens, berries and this tea is a very good diet under most conditions.

Roots and young shoots of cattails are a good source of food. They are mostly protein. You may remove the pollen from the middle of the stem, dry it, making it into a crude flour to make biscuits. The inner bark of many trees such as aspen, willow, birch or any cone-bearing tree is edible. The inner bark may be eaten immediately or dried and cooked later. This is one of your most reliable sources of plant food.

Most blue and black berries are edible. Do not eat red, and especially white berries as they are mostly poisonous. Stay away from plants that look and smell like beans, cucumbers, melons, carrots or parsnips, as most are extremely poisonous. Absolutely, do not eat any plants that resemble parsely, dill or smell like them. Just because you see an animal eating these plants does not mean a human can consume them. Another good source of food is filberts, walnuts, and acorns.

You can hunt frogs but stay away from salamanders as they are very poisonous. Remove the frog's legs and boil, fry or roast them. You can snare or shoot all birds as they are all edible. Pick them, do not skin them as you need to keep all the fat you can in the outer tissue. All fish are edible. In the case of carp, though, after filleting them, cut away all the red meat and cook only the white meat. All very small fish, like smelt, may be eaten bones and all, but do not eat the heads. However, keep the heads to make a nourishing soup. You can boil, bake or roast all fish, but it is desirable to boil them. After boiling the fish, drink the water as the broth has all the nutrients lost in cooking as well as all the water intake you will need.

Grasshoppers, grubs, worms and ants are also good sources of protein. Remove the heads, legs and wings and bake the bodies between leaves in the coals of the fire. Ants are not worth the time and trouble to collect.

Snakes and lizards are edible. Cut the heads off, remove the entrails and peel the skin as you would a banana. They are ready for cooking. All mice, grey diggers, squirrels, rabbits and porcupines can provide meat. Prepare as you would a rabbit — skinning and quartering them. Check the animals carefully for sores as this is a tell-tale sign of disease. These animals should not be eaten. All meat should be cooked fully.

Prevention is utmost to wilderness survival. One of the last things we need to discuss is hygiene. As a practical rule, keep yourself as clean as possible. It is very important to keep clean, but your underwear and socks are most important. If you have no soap, beating your clothes on a rock in water will be sufficient for a short time. Again, take special care of your feet as without them you will not be able to forage for food and water.

While out hunting you must take a hot shower (if possible) every three days and keep your clothes clean or the deer will surely smell you. No amount of cover scent will ever cover three days of body odor. The era of the mountain man is gone!

A toothbrush may be made by chewing a green twig. Use aspirin if you have no toothpaste and be sure to scrub your teeth gently as not to cause bleeding; be sure to rinse your mouth with water.

In hot weather avoid being sunburned; in cold weather avoid frostbite on your hands, feet, fingers and ears. Avoid contact with mosquitoes, flies, lice and ticks as they can carry serious diseases. Blisters are dangerous as they can cause infections. A good pair of boots or shoes that fit well and clean socks will prevent most foot blisters.

Most first aid kits have the basic supplies you will need, but are a little expensive so we prefer to make up our own.

Some problems you might run into while out on your trip are "BURNS" — most are first or second degree. The treatment is to put the area in cool clean water and clean it carefully. If blisters are present, do not break them. Clean them gently and wrap them in a clean cloth.

"DIARRHEA" is difficult to treat without any baregoric medicine. The best treatment is to stop eating for twenty-four hours but do drink small amounts of water during the day to replace fluids lost. Dehydration is a danger at this time. Continue this until the symptoms stop.

With "HYPOTHERMIA" try to get dry as soon as possible. Get warm by a fire or with blankets to ease the chills that come with hypothermia. You may use warm liquids to bring your body temperature up. Doing this will make the danger pass easier.

"BEE STINGS" are one of the most common problems you will encounter. Unless you are allergic to them, they pose a very small hazard. If you are stung you should look to see if the stinger is in your skin. If so, take your hand and gently brush it away. Do not try to pinch or pull it out as it will break the stinger off and force more poison into you. After the stinger has been removed try to find some mud to put on the wound. The mud will help draw the poison and ease the swelling.

"POISONOUS SNAKE BITES" are very rare. Rattlesnakes are the only ones you need to fear in eastern Oregon. To prevent this problem, watch where you put your hands while climbing. Remember snakes are slow moving in the morning, but in the afternoon and later in the day the snake will be hunting and you should be careful at this time. Most snakebite kits do more harm than good. As snakes feed on mice, most of the time you will not die from the snakebite (unless you are allergic to them) but you will be very sick. Try to obtain professional help as soon as possible.

F. TOPOGRAPHICAL MAPS/HANDMADE MAPS

The next time you look at a topo map, see how much useable detail is shown. Some are so full of lines you cannot distinguish between creeks, roads, trails and elevation lines. On picture 2-C you can see the advantages of a handmade map. Without it you do not see the beaver ponds on either side of where your camp has been made, or other landmarks. In picture 2-C on this topo map you will see a dark lined square. In the lower right hand section, you can count 18 squares which are one-mile squares. You see two major trails that run through the map lines. Some are horse trails and some are foot trails. You cannot tell the difference between these lines until you look at the trailhead marker. Creek names are a big asset to indicate your location, but there are no markers on the creeks in the wilderness. Look at figure 2-C and you will see a major highway in the top right corner. If you were to be scouting, this is the road you would come in on. That is where you will begin your exploration of a new area to hunt. A topo map has a sufficient amount of detail to explore your new hunting areas.

On your first trip, look for the best campsight. You may also mark deer sightings and where you might have harvested a deer before. This information may be used to map deer movement in the future. To aid in picking a wilderness area, we have compiled a list of the wilderness areas in Oregon, in alphabetical order. They are: (1) Diamond Peak Wilderness in the Willamette National Forest; (2) Eagle Cap Wilderness in the Willowa-Whitman Forest; (3) Gearheart Wilderness in the Fremont National Forest; (4) Mt. Hood Wilderness in the Mt. Hood National Forest; (5) Mt. Jefferson Wilderness in the Willamette National Forest; (6) Kalmiopsis Wilderness in the Siskiyou National Forest; (7) Mtn. Lakes Wilderness in the Rogue River National Forest; (8) The Strawberry Mt. Wilderness in the Malheur National Forest; (9)

The Three Sisters Wilderness in the Deschutes National Forest; and (10) Mt. Washington Wilderness in the Willamette National Forest.

If you want to hunt other states for trophy class deer, let us suggest these states. The state of Utah has good numbers of class bucks. You may call the Dept. of Fish and Game at 1-801-538-4700 in Salt Lake City. Try asking about these three areas: High Uintas Primitive area in the Wasatch National Forest or the Dark Canyon Primitive area in the Manli-la sal National Forest and the Grand Gulch Primitive area in the National Bridges National Forest.

Another choice is Idaho. To find out about out-of-state tags and such, call 1-208-334-3717 Boise. Look into these areas: the Bitterroot Range in the Coeur d'Alene National Forest or the Gospel Hump Wilderness area in the Nez Perce National Forest and last, the Sawtooth Wilderness area in the Sawtooth National Forest.

Our last suggestion is the state of Montana. For out-of-state information call 1-406-542-5500 Missoula. Try to acquire maps for the Gates of the Mountains Wilderness area in the Helena National Forest and you can look at the Bitterroot Range in the Beaverhead National Forest. The Bitterroot Range is on the border between Idaho and Montana. There is one more place and that is also in the Beaverhead National Forest. It is the Red Rock Lakes National Wilderness area. All these areas have deer and are worth looking into for future hunts. And there are also the states of Colorado and Wyoming but we have no experience hunting these states.

In these locations try to look for places where horse packers are excluded or you will have to compete against them since they can cover the ground faster than you can and you may be hunting areas that they have already hunted.

This sleek blacktail buck's velvet-covered antlers are almost fully grown.

CHAPTER 3

CAMPING AND HUNTING GEAR

A. CAMPING AND HUNTING GEAR

Most people have accumulated gear over a period of time. As you need to add equipment now and then, or if you are considering changing your hunting tactics, here are some ways to save money and still get the equipment you need.

You might want to get a new sleeping bag. If so, look at the rating on the bag, then evaluate the temperatures for the time of year you are going to be camping. We prefer to use a light-weight sleeping bag and an extra blanket. You can wash the sleeping bags at a laundromat. If the inside comes apart you can stitch it up with a large needle and thread or sew an old sheet to the edge of the sleeping bag on the sewing machine. If you plan to leave your gear in camp for any length of time, try purchasing it at a thrift store or a garage sale. By doing this, if someone runs off with it while you are out of camp you will not be out a lot of money. Even though we leave our camp unattended for some period of time, we have had no problem with anyone taking anything from our camp.

We have some thoughts to share with you as you begin to choose your cooking gear. We prefer to purchase our cooking gear at thrift stores or garage sales. Try to stay away from aluminum kits. Almost everything sticks to aluminum while cooking. They will also warp and burn up if used on an open fire for any length of time. Cast iron or stainless steel pots and pans are very durable. However, we prefer Teflon coated skillets, pots and pans. It is difficult to find Teflon coated skillets in good condition at the thrift stores but the regular stores usually have these skillets for a reasonable price.

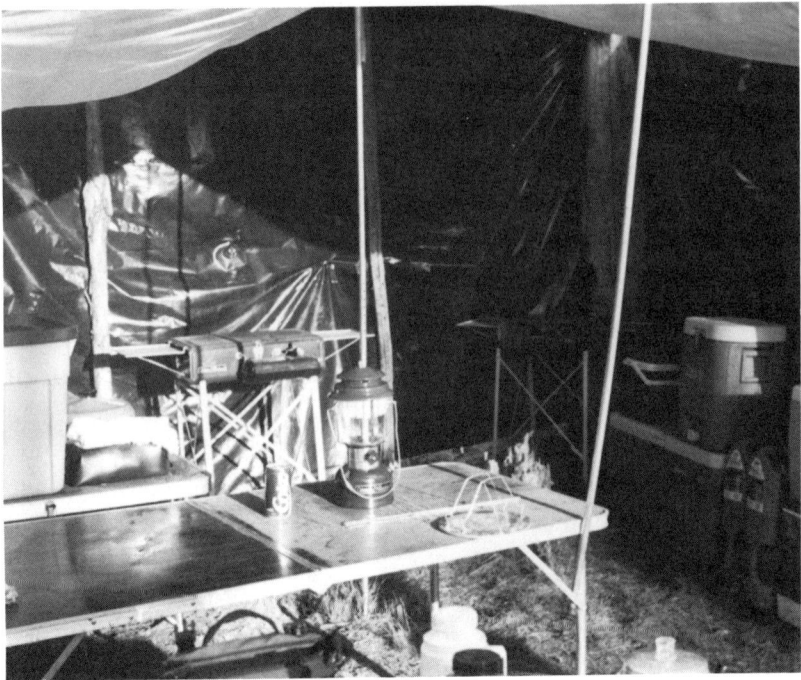

Photo 3A

Be sure to purchase two extra sets of silverware. The silverware will not usually be matched, but it is by far cheaper to purchase at the thrift store.

Purchase butter knives with serrated edges as they will serve also as steak knives.

Coffee cups may either be the enamel cups, which are expensive, or plastic cups. Try to stay away from aluminum cups as they leave a metal taste in your mouth.

Remove the handles from the skillets you purchased.

Cut a broom handle and taper it to fit the ends of each skillet. Take a hacksaw and, about 1/2 inch from the end of each piece of handle, cut a straight line about 1/4 inch deep. Make an angle cut to intersect the other leaving a notch; drill a hole in the notch to fit the bolt of the skillet, then put the wooden handle on the skillet. Make the handles a little longer than the original handle, about 1 1/2 to 2 times the original handle length. Attach a small hook to the end so you can hang them up to dry after washing them.

When choosing salad bowls, get plastic ones as they are more durable.

Water containers are found in either hard plastic or collapsible ones. If the water tastes like plastic you may mix some baking soda with water then rinse the container the next day. In time, doing this will sweeten the taste of the water.

Picture 3-A shows an assortment of camping gear we have accumulated over the years. We bought some of the gear new and some used.

B. BACKPACKING GEAR

Backpacking is more fun than ever today! With new technology and equipment you can go deeper into the backpacking territory than in the past.

If your party only backpacks on weekends, you should use the amount of gear that you can carry in and out on one trip. If you have never been backpacking, we would like to help you put together your equipment. The first item you will need to purchase is the backpack itself. The largest pack I have seen was a 5,000 square inch one. It would accommodate 150 pounds of equipment.

When you look for a pack you will need to use a formula to allow you to carry the right amount of weight for each person. We have come up with a formula that we use which consists of measuring the square inches and converting it into approximate pounds the space will accommodate. Most all packs have a square inch rating label on them. When purchasing a backpack try not to purchase one too large or too small for your needs. Some dealers will be able to assist you. If you have no qualified dealer to help you, we can help you with the formula we use to pick pack sizes for each of us. Considering a normal pack load with clothes, food, cooking supplies, fishing and hunting equipment, sleeping and survival gear, etc., the square inch rule works out to about a 5 inch by 5 inch by 5 inch square, which is equal to approximately 4 pounds of gear. As far as design of a pack, we do not consider using any pack that does not have a frame. It is imperative to have a frame to support and distribute the weight down on your lower hips. Loading the pack with heavy goods at the bottom of the pack will help do this. The higher the weight is placed in the pack the more back strain it will cause.

We have no preference between metal or plastic frames. Both are adequate and equally functional. We have noticed there are more plastic framed packs today than metal ones because of the strength and lightness of the space age plastic developed in the recent years. As far as canvas versus nylon, the only difference is that nylon does not rot as canvas does if it is stored when wet. There is one difference in the packs that is worth mentioning. The conventional kind we call the top loader and the newer kind we call the front loader. The top loader is the easier loading of the two, but the front loader is easier to remove something from while on the packing trail or in an emergency.

If your hunts are going to be weekend trips, the front loader is your best choice. You may lay it down and unzip it and almost everything in the pack can be taken out without disturbing the rest of the items. For week long trips and for packing out meat, the top loader is best because you can pack it tighter than the front loader. Color of a pack is a personal preference. Some packs have many compartments. They are best used on top loaders as usually the things you need are always on the bottom. Using these compartments to load items such as your first aid kit will allow you to get to it quickly. A

The newer front-loader packs are an improvement over the old-style top loaders.

front loader has a zipper on the front shaped in a "U". After it is unzipped you can see everything in the pack. Try several packs and ask the salesperson for help in adjusting the straps. Don't forget our formula and look for the correct size to fit your needs.

There are many tents on the market today such as the Boy Scouts' type tent, the light dome tent or the traditional four-man frame tent and the large wall tent. When checking ratings on tents, if the tent is rated as a four man tent, consider it a two man tent. Decide before leaving on your trip whether each person is to carry his own tent or if you all are going to share one large tent. If your tent is not waterproof, spray it with some water repellent spray or develop a rain fly out of a piece of plastic.

Your tent dealer may help you decide which tent is right for your type of use.

Cooking paraphernalia can be found in most thrift stores. Some things you might look for are an old barbecue grill or a rack out of a refrigerator. It can be cut to a desired size with a hacksaw to fit in a backpack. A two foot by two foot size grate is about the right size for most uses over a firepit cooking area. One item that can be used for water storage is a one liter soda pop jug. After washing them out, tie a small piece of string around the neck and hang them on the outside of your backpack. You should have at least one jug per person for a weekend trip.

If your trip is going to be longer than a weekend, you should return to town every three days to wash clothes and get fresh provisions.

Do not try to carry everything you will need for a week's stay as you will never be able to carry it all.

C. FANNYPACK ITEMS

Your fannypack will be your life's blood while hunting. Hopefully you will not forget any vital pieces of it or it may be a fatal mistake.

When backpacking, no matter where you go, even to the bathroom, your fannypack should go with you. Remember it should always be some place where you will not leave it behind or you will be in danger. If anyone thinks I am kidding, he is a fool. Anyone who has backpacked for any length of time will go without a coat or a hat or even without their map but never without their fannypack.

In our fannypacks you will find in every pouch a small box of wooden matches, and in some we have waterproof matches. In the large compartments you will find a saw, one piece of plastic (six by six feet square), a small axhead, some parachute cord, 5 nails, a small file, twelve feet of 10 lb. fishing line, two spools of 6 lb. leader, 12 hooks, and a vial of lead, a small jar of fishing eggs, three floats and a supply of flies. You will also find a spool of snare wire, one bottle of water purification tablets, a small pot, some packages of dried soups, two space survival blankets, one candle, and two emergency flares. Some people will carry a Boy Scout knife or a Swiss army knife, a first aid kit, a map of your hunting area and a compass. We also take a couple of granola bars and two tea bags, (as far as candy bars, stay away from the chocolate kind.) Nut rolls are better and they do not melt like the others. Popcorn is another good item as it takes up very little space. A small amount of honey is a topping that can be put over the popcorn to make a complete and nutritious meal. You will need two pair of socks, a small bar of soap, some toilet paper, and a couple of small plastic bags.

I am sure your fannypack will include some of these things and some I have not mentioned. Everyone must put together his own pack for their peace of mind.

D. BUYING YOUR HUNTING GEAR

One item you will have trouble finding will be a pair of galoshes to fit over your shoes. The reason we use rubber is that it does not allow human odor to penetrate. This makes your movements across the ground scent proof to the deer. If you cannot find any galoshes, look for a pair of rubber soled boots or tennis shoes. You should coat any boot or galosh with a cover scent such as earth scent, pine scent or cedar. All work well.

Binoculars are a very important item. They should be as small and light as possible. Most binoculars are 7x35. The numbers on the binoculars have a meaning. The first number refers to the power of magnification compared to your eyes. Meaning, the binoculars have seven times the power as your eyes. The second number refers to the size of the large lens on the front of the binoculars. This also determines how much width perception you will have. You will find other sizes such as 8x25, 10x50 and so on. In our type of hunting we spend 90% of the time in one spot. We need to be looking for small parts of a deer through the brush so we prefer a little more power but less field of vision. Be sure to use a neck strap as, if you drop the binoculars, they are usually broken.

Now we are into a subject that is very personal — a

knife. We prefer a slender, pointed knife with a strong blade. This type is great for cleaning fish and opening paunches of deer. But if that is not the kind you like, as long as your knife holds an edge and feels good in your hand, use it. As far as folding knives versus one-piece knives, we use both. Make sure the knife has a good locking device so as not to cut your fingers. I personally carry a one-piece knife in a leather sheath. The length of the blade is a matter of preference. We prefer a 5 to 7 inch blade because it is easy to work with in the cavity of the deer. Most beginners start with too big of a knife.

E. BOOTS VERSUS CAMO BOOTS

If you hunt in the wet weather the Gortex lined leather boot might be for you. It allows foot perspiration to escape but keeps water out. Wet feet are a disaster on any hunting trip. Normally I like to have two pair of boots so I can change boots every day. This allows the boots to completely dry out. If they do not, the leather will rot.

Most of our party hunt in the dry eastern part of our state. The early bow season is usually hot and dry. High-top tennis shoes is what all of us use on our hunts. The tennis shoe you pick should be some kind of camo and have a semi-soft sole. In dry country, while trying to move over dry twigs and leaves, you must have a soft touch. Some hunters have been known to hunt in a double pair of socks but we are wary of snakes.

If you hunt out of a tree stand the first thing a deer will see is your feet and legs. It is imperative to wear camo shoes. No matter which you choose, make sure they are broken in as sore feet will ruin the hunt.

F. SAWS

Now for a little information on saws. There are two kinds of packsaws. The one-bladed folding saw is good for cutting wood but is difficult to cut meat with. When folded up it is safe to pack as the blade goes inside the handle and the teeth are covered completely. The second saw is a two-sided T-saw. One side has large teeth for wood cutting and the other side has small teeth which work well for bone sawing. You must keep all saws oiled and in sheaths or they will rust and dull quickly. Most saws come with a leather or nylon case. Either case is sufficient to protect you from the sharp teeth.

G. DEER BAGS

There are two types of deer bags on the market today — the cheesecloth kind and the sheet kind. The cheesecloth will keep meat clean but flies can still touch the meat between the weave in the cheesecloth. This may allow them to lay eggs in the meat and cause spoilage. It does allow good air flow but I prefer to use the sheet kind. If I am not going to bone my animal, the sheet allows for a tighter weave and protects the meat better from flies and from dirt. Hanging your deer in one of these sheet cloths will allow the deer to age but keep it in a locker if you can.

H. GUN AND BOW CHOICES

We will not go into ballistics of ammo as there are better books regarding this subject than I can describe in this small chapter. Look at picture 3-C you will see the differences in ammo sizes.

We do have some advice on guns and ammo starting with the most common gun which is the 30/30. This is an excellent choice if the person is small or just beginning to hunt. But it should be bought in a bolt action for the beginning hunter.

The 30/30 caliber can also be bought in several brands. We do feel that the side ejection guns are a better choice because these guns eject the shell out of the side of the gun, whereas others eject the shell out the top. If you want to put a scope on a top ejector gun, you must mount the scope on a side mount which is difficult for the beginner to use as the head and eye are off to the side when aiming. The side ejectors use a standard set of rings and mounts and are mounted directly on top. The 30/30 caliber is a very accurate rifle but it should be used at close distances. The average shooter can shoot this gun between 84 and 100 yards maximum. If you are hunting brushy terrain, this gun is adequate. More deer have been killed with a 30/30 than any other rifle because there are so many in use.

The next choice is a 25/06. A 25 caliber has better velocity and range than a 30/30. It also has a good choice of ballistics as far as ammo is concerned. It comes in bolt, automatic, or lever action. If buying a rifle for a beginner, I prefer to give them a bolt or lever action as it is basically a single shot. No matter who uses any gun, they should be familiar with the way the gun works, loads and unloads.

The third choice is the 300 Savage. It is a 30 caliber and I personally prefer shooting this gun. It shoots a small bullet with a large powder charge. It has higher velocity but it does not spoil much meat when it comes out the other side of the deer like some of the heavier weight guns do.

Let's examine the heavier weight guns. The first is the 308 Winchester. It is also a 30 caliber. Most women and young men prefer this gun in the heavy-weight class as it shoots hard and accurate at longer distances, but still has a somewhat light recoil.

The second choice is a 270 Winchester. This gun packs a wallop. It is the main choice of many men that deer hunt. It will shoot as accurately at any distance as any gun, providing you shoot the correct load.

The most popular caliber gun shot today, and my absolute favorite heavy-weight gun, is the 30/06 rifle. This is my choice over all the heavy-weight guns. The 30/06 can shoot accurately from 100 to 300 yards depending on the person shooting. It also comes in bolt action, lever or automatic. One advantage the gun has is that you can buy a wide range of bullet sizes and powder grain differences over-the-counter.

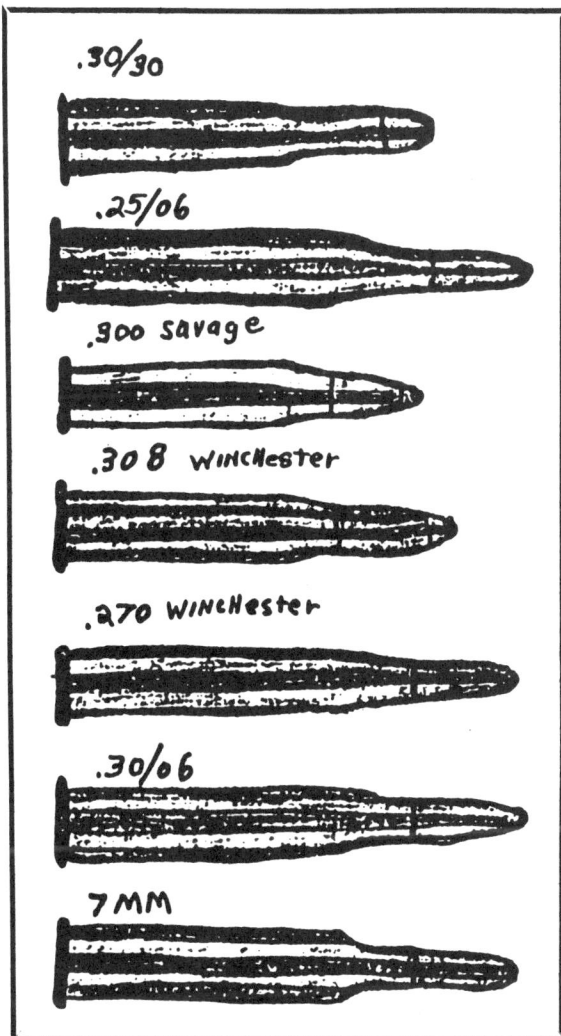

Illustration 3C

Another good point that I need to bring to your attention is, if you are ever in need of ammo on a hunt and you are in a small-town store, most of the time they will have two calibers — the 30/30 and the 30/06. If you can handle the recoil, the 30/06 is the best all around choice. The bullet shapes for this caliber are Corelock, pointed soft point and blunt nose. The powder grains will run 110 grains, 150 grains and 220 grains. I prefer the pointed soft point because it mushrooms as it goes out the other side of the animal allowing for a variance in shot placement and still has a high kill factor. This particular bullet will go in one side the size of a dime and will come out the other side the size of your fist. I do sometimes shoot a 300 Savage but when I do, I prefer to shoot a silver-tipped bullet. We call it the "werewolf" bullet. It also mushrooms but not as much as the pointed soft point does. Do try to shoot at least three or more calibers before you choose the gun you want.

We shoot factory loaded ammo exclusively because in a standard load we have never had a failure of any kind. If you look at factory machinery for reloading, you can easily see it is top-of-the-line. Compare it with the reloading equipment you can buy in the store which is primitive by comparison. Unless you are going to shoot more than 20 boxes a year and want to spend the time to learn how to reload correctly, you are safer and money ahead to shoot the factory loads.

After transporting a gun, I like to test fire it once on a six inch pie plate target. If it is still shooting in the center I am confident of the accuracy.

The bolt action is the most accurate shooting action of the three most popular guns.

After choosing the caliber of gun you want, add a scope to it and then have the gun bore sighted. There is a big myth about bore sighting a gun. When a gun is bore sighted, the center of the barrel is lined up with crosshairs in the scope. This in no way means the gun is sighted-in as most people think. The rifling in the barrel will cause a bullet to spin and as it comes out of the gun, the centrifugal force will wobble the bullet slightly. The bore sighting will get your first shots on the paper target. Without bore sighting, you might shoot 5 to 20 shells and never know where the gun is shooting. Any gun that is going to be shot at a deer should be able to keep three consecutive bullets in a three inch circle at 100 yards. Here are some reasons why.

Each gun will shoot a certain bullet grain weight size more accurately than any other size. This is due to the construction of this particular gun. A dealer can assist you in picking a grain weight bullet. Just tell him what you are going to hunt and how far you need to shoot and he should be able to help you pick the correct bullet. Before you go out to sight in your gun, purchase four boxes of ammo. Shells do not spoil but ammo from year to year will vary in performance somewhat, sometimes as much as three inches one way or the other. Next get two pairs of blue jeans, sew up the bottom legs, fill each side with sand about eight inches long, sew up that side, cut them apart to make four sand bags. Cut two four by four wood blocks eight inches long. You will also need an old table and a chair. Take these items with you unless you are going to a regulation shooting range. Place a sandbag on top of one four by four block. Rest the forearm of the gun on this. Take another sandbag or two and place them below the butt of the gun. Look through the scope and try to align the crosshairs in the center of the target. Without touching the gun, the crosshairs should sit in the center of the target. The target should be a 3-inch white circle. Without moving the gun, place your shoulder up against the butt of the gun. Shoot the gun one time. Approach the target and physically see where you shot. Mark this hole with a number one and a circle around it. Return to the gun and shoot it again. Mark the hole with a two and a circle around it. Shoot a third time and check it the same way.

Remove the scope and adjustment covers. The top screw will be the elevation. The windage screw will be on the side and is marked L and R. A dime will work well as a turning tool. Usually, each click will be 1/4 or 1/8 of an inch increment.

After you feel your windage adjustment has been corrected, give the scope a hit with the palm of your hand on the side of the scope — not hard — but enough so that the cross hairs in the scope, if hung up, will fall in place. After allowing the barrel to cool for 15 minutes you may shoot the gun again as before. Remember, if you do not allow the 15 minutes for the barrel to cool, it will continue to warp. The holes in the target will do what we call roundhouse, meaning that the gun will continue to shoot holes around the center of the target and never settle in one spot. When I sight-in guns I usually take three or four guns with me. I also take one piece of paper to write down where the first gun is shooting. After shooting the first gun and making the adjustments, I set it aside. I then shoot the second gun, make the adjustments and set it behind the first, rotating the guns as the 15 minute time period elapses.

When the gun is correctly sighted-in, you should be able to place all three shots in a three-inch circle at 100 yards. The reason for shooting the guns with a cold barrel is that the first shot at a deer will be with a cold barrel and that is the shot we want to be accurate. There is nothing you can do about a hot barrel warping. It is worth the time invested to pre-shoot your guns rather than to talk about the big one you missed.

The bow is the weapon of our choice. It is one of the most difficult ways to harvest a deer, but one of the most rewarding. Begin with your target and backstop. The backstop should never be grass hay or straw. The grass hay or straw will allow the arrows to pass through and will tear off the feathers or vanes. We prefer to use a portable high density foam target or cedar bales.

To get started, go to a pro shop and have your draw length measured. Your draw length is how far you draw the bow back to the anchor point on the side of your face. Remember, at your anchor point you will feel the 50% or 65% let off, meaning your holding weight is much less than the shooting weight. Examine figure 3-D to see the three types of bows used by today's bow hunters.

When examining different bows you will notice there are more metal-handled ones than wood. There are two kinds of limbs; one is made of laminated wood and the other is made of fiberglass. Both have advantages and disadvantages. Fiberglass is very tough. It is impervious to heat and water as much as any limb can possibly be. The laminated wood limbs are not as tough as fiberglass but wood laminated limbs have a good characteristic. They are traditionally faster than fiberglass limbs. Both, occasionally, have limb failures, although the fiberglass is the least likely to have limb failure. In limb construction there are straight limbs and recurved limbs. The difference in the two limbs is that the recurved limbs store the energy better than the straight limbs. They are traditionally a little smoother in shooting than the straight limbs but in most cases are not as fast as the straight limbs.

You may notice the differences in the wheels. Some have round wheels and some have egg-shaped wheels which are called a cam. The cam is a little more difficult to draw than the wheel but it will shoot an arrow 15 feet a second faster than the wheel bow at the same poundage. However, the wheel is easier to draw and more forgiving in the mistakes

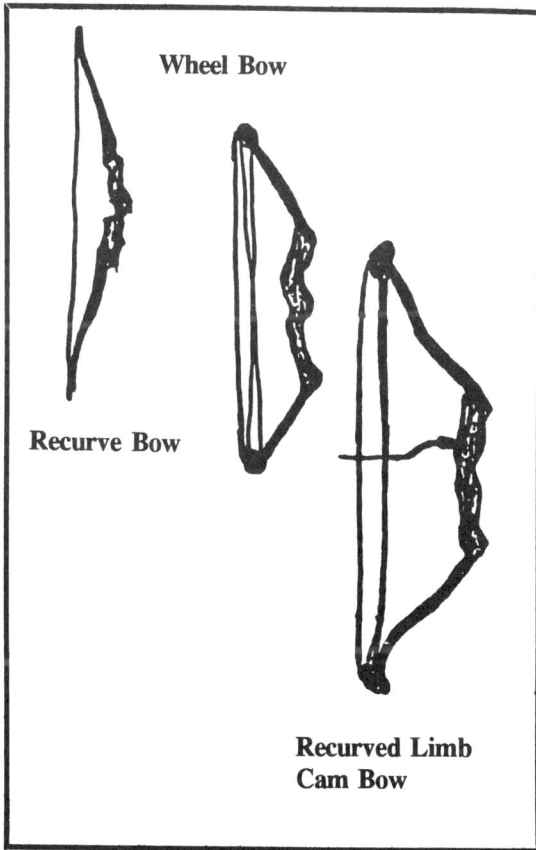

Illustration 3D

made in shooting form.

Another feature to look at is the length of the bow. If you draw 29 inches or less you can shoot just about any bow you want without problems of string pinch. But if your draw is 30 inches or more, you should shoot a fairly long-limbed bow. At least 50 inches of bow measured from tip to tip or from axle to axle is considered a long bow. As you draw the bow the string is shaped in a V. With short-limbed bows you have a short axle to axle bow.

The string V becomes very severe but with a longer bow the V is less severe as the axles are farther apart. The problems you will encounter are that your fingers on the short V's will become sore the more you shoot because of the severity of the angle of the string against your fingers. This does not occur with the longer axled bows. Another problem is that with the short axle to axle bows the arrow is put at an angle on the string in such a manner that it is not locked securely on the string. The arrow can slip off the string as you shoot. This causes a dryfire, which can break the bow.

Not many recurve bows are in circulation. They are used by about one out of every five shooters. The long bows are used even less. The disadvantage of these two style bows is they are very difficult to draw and hold at your anchor point. This will cause problems in release. It is inadvisable for the beginner to hunt with the long bow as you also will not have any sights on it making you very inaccurate. Do not let someone advise you to start shooting without sights which is called instinctive shooting. It takes much practice — usually more time than you have before hunting season begins. Our philosophy is "you do not shoot a gun without sights so why would you shoot a bow without sights?"

The way you move the pin will make you shoot the opposite. Keep moving the pin and shooting until you can hit the target in the center while holding the pin in the center of the bullseye.

If you have any other problems consult your dealer as there might be a problem with some part of the equipment.

When you begin looking at arrows, you will notice most of the arrows are aluminum. The smallest hunting shaft made is an 18/16. The largest shaft you can buy is a 24/19, meaning this shaft is 24mm outside diameter and 19mm wall thickness. The proper wall thickness is called the "spline."

If you shoot a shaft with too thin of a wall thickness, the arrow, when it comes out of the bow, flexes too many times and never stabilizes. Ideally, you want the shaft to flex approximately four times and then you want the flexing motion to cease. When the fletch starts to turn the shaft it makes the arrow fly like a bullet.

If you shoot a too heavily splined arrow, the shaft only flexes once or twice. The flexing motion then stops. The fletch tries to turn the shaft but the arrow is still at an angle. As the fletch turns the shaft the arrow begins to wobble and at a short distance it will fall like a rock. Your dealer should be able to pick the correct arrow for the bow you are shooting.

When you choose broadheads, if you are shooting 40 pounds to 49 pounds, try to pick a broadhead that is three-bladed and weighs from 90 to 110 grains. At 50 pounds to 60 pounds, try to pick a broadhead that is also three-bladed and weighs from 125 to 135 grains. At about 70 pounds, you will need a broadhead that is either three or four bladed and weighs from 145 to 180 grains. After shooting many different broadheads and various weights, we discovered that the four-bladed broadheads are aerodynamically unstable at lower poundages. You must shoot a broadhead to determine if it is going to fly out of your bow correctly.

Trying a different broadhead is one answer if the arrow doesn't fly correctly. The other answer is to tune your equipment to shoot that broadhead. When trying to tune your equipment to the broadhead, you can only do a few things. First, you can go up or down in arrow spline or you can go from three-fletched arrows to four-fletched arrows. The only difference the four-fletched arrows will make is that it will spin the arrow faster. The arrow will fly a tad bit slower but will be more accurate. If this does not solve the problem, the only other option is to fletch your arrows in feathers rather than plastic vanes. The feather is more stable and more forgiving in shooting form mistakes than the plastic vane. Using a four-fletched feather is the most traditional way to stablize your arrows. Other than lowering or raising the poundage on your bow, there is nothing else you can do to get a broadhead to fly correctly. You will hear people say feathered arrows are not durable. These people, in our opinion, are wrong. The feather, when wet, does have a problem flying. I personally have shot an arrow into a creek, submerging it completely under water, and left it there for a few minutes. After retrieving the arrow I blew the moisture off. Returning it to my quiver I continued to shoot other targets. After four minutes I reknocked the same arrow, shot it and it flew perfectly. A feather, given time to dry, and especially if it has been treated with some form of spray silicone, will perform perfectly after being very wet.

When shooting your bow for practice, you will shoot a field point which is a practice head. About two weeks before hunting season put your broadheads on your arrows and tune your equipment so that your broadheads fly accurately and smoothly to the target. The broadhead will not fly the same as a field point. You must shoot the broadhead and tune for the broadhead before you hunt with it, as you will not be able to purchase feathered arrows from most stores. You may be able to have them made, or custom made, at a pro shop — or you may purchase a fletching jig and do it yourself. With this tool you will not only be able to fletch feathers or vanes but you will be able to change color, size and four-fletch or three-fletch. We prefer to shoot bright colored fletching on our practice arrows and darker colored fletching on our hunting arrows. But we always shoot a brightly colored nock. Arrows can be fletched in left helical or right helical or straight. The helical arrow does catch the wind a little faster. It stabilizes the arrow usually faster with a broadhead on it. Most shooters shoot a helical of some kind.

The way to tune to a broadhead is to take three straight arrows, put two field points on two of them and a broadhead on the third and shoot all three arrows. See if the one with the broadhead flies high, low, left or right from the two with field points on them. Then make the adjustment on the sight to compensate and allow you to hit the target in the center at various distances with the broadhead arrow. When you go back to the field point for practice later in the season, you will need to adjust your sights so that you can hit the target with the field points. Most of the time the broadhead will pick you, you will not pick the broadhead.

There is a vast variety of quivers to choose from. If you are hunting close to camp you may choose a four arrow quiver. Most people will try to keep their bow as light as possible as the bow gets heavy when you pack it all day. If you are going to the bottom of a canyon and are going to spend most of the day there, try to choose a seven to nine arrow quiver. I personally have never shot more than four or five arrows in one day. After you have set up your equipment, try to shoot some 3-D trail shoots if possible. They are hosted by archery clubs in the area. Most shoots will say 3-D on them, meaning the targets are life size. Most of them are taxidermy molds with real horns on them. This is the best practice you can have next to actually hunting live deer. What you will learn at these shoots is how to judge distance in the woods, which is the number one reason most deer are missed each year. Looking at a deer from the side there is only 18 inches of space in which you can hit a deer but the vital kill area is actually only 6 inches in height.

These targets are placed so that you will be shooting at all angles and through small openings, between trees and up and down hills. Your skill as a shooter with the technical equipment you are using will show up almost immediately. Some shoots also have moving targets. Most of the time people will not shoot at a running deer. But under certain conditions, some people will shoot. These targets will teach you how poor a running shot is under hunting conditions.

I shot a deer the second year I bow hunted. It was a little forked antlered deer that had come within ten feet of me.

I was so excited that when I pulled up to shoot, I chose my favorite rifle shot — the neck shot. This is a poor choice for a bowhunter but I didn't know this. I learned bowhunting the hard way — making a lot of mistakes. The deer fell, got up and ran off as fast as he could. Not believing my eyes, I started after him immediately — another mistake. I saw him again, once. He was looking my way. The moment his eyes met mine, he was gone for good. I looked the rest of the day. He was nowhere to be found.

I was so embarrassed I told no one in camp what had happened that day. The next day I was looking over the spot where I had hit the little buck. I pondered the direction I had seen him travel. I decided to follow a small ravine down and allow my eyes to guide my direction, putting myself in the buck's dilemma of needing to run but not having the strength to go uphill. After going a good distance, I stopped to look the ground over. I looked at a log about six or eight feet away and noticed something light colored hanging from it. It was rather wet looking. Before I took more than two steps, I realized what I was looking at. It was a piece of my deer's windpipe and some saliva covered with blood. A chill went up and down my back. This had to be my buck. I saw stumbling marks leading down and around the hill but I was still unable to locate the deer. Starting out again the next day I climbed to a vantage point where I noticed some birds circling not far from where my trail ended the day before. Hurrying over to the spot I started to search again. I found my buck in the bottom of a deep canyon. He was bloated and unfit to eat. I apologized to him for his suffering and vowed to be a more efficient hunter with a bow. I would always prefer to miss a deer than wound him. At that moment I said, "You are the deer I shot and you are the deer I will tag." I took his head from his body and I returned to camp. I placed the small buck's head at the meat pole. Only one person asked about the head with no body. The people in camp knew me well and with a low tone I said it was mine. People scattered every which way and I never heard another word about the head again.

Some people would ask, "What purpose did it achieve to put my tag on such a small buck, especially when I did not get any meat from it?" I still have the rack of this deer today and after each season I reminisce on how this little buck made me a better hunter. I hope this story will keep you from making these types of errors.

This display of Jim and Wes Brown's antlers appears at many sportsman shows in the western states.

CHAPTER 4

BUILDING CAMPS

A. SHELTER BUILDING

Whether you are hunting or scouting roaded areas, or backpacking, you need a place where your party can gather and socialize while being protected from the elements. Picture 4-A shows the type of shelter we have used for many years. Its construction is very simple. With just a few items and with a little help anyone can build this type of structure in about two hours. How large you construct your shelter depends on party size and what it will be used for. On one side of our shelter we always build a kitchen (see pictures 4-B and 4-C). You need not build a big shelter — an 8 foot by 8 foot space is adequate. At our camp we use our shelter to base our backpacking trips into the deeper wilderness. Picture 4-D shows the framework being assembled. Picture 4-E shows the same shelter completed. The sideview shows the angle of the roof and how the fire pit and tables are placed in and around the shelter. When looking for a good campsite, try to be a reasonable distance away from the water. This will avoid the mosquitoes and other bugs that make camp life unbearable. When beginning construction on your shelter you will need a few tools and materials such as a spring loaded staple gun and staples, 200 yards of parachute cord, a small ax, a sack of nails, a wood handsaw, some gray duct tape, two rolls of black plastic, 25 feet by 10 feet, 30 feet of cardboard strips 2" wide, a small leaf rake, a sharp knife, two round 5 or 7 gallon plastic buckets and a shovel.

We will show you how to build a shelter to accommodate four people. (It doesn't matter if the four corner

Illustration 4A

supports aren't perfectly square.) For four people you will need 144 square feet, which is a 12 x 12 foot space. Rake all the debris you can from within the area. Move this debris to a pile west of the shelter. This material will be used to start fires as it is dry and very easy to ignite. You will need to cut ten poles long enough to span the distance between the trees and you will need nine poles eight feet long. Using the plastic buckets to stand on, start on the back side first. Cut the parachute cord in a length that allows you to go around the tree and the poles twice like an X, leaving enough to tie a square knot. Poles should not be more than three inches in diameter at the small end. The length of the poles should be three to six inches beyond the four corner trees. (The reason we tie the poles is that you are not allowed by law, in most states, to nail or screw anything into a live tree.) Take a pole and tie it about six feet high on the east side trees. The poles go on the outside of the trees. Now move to the west end and secure the poles in the same manner but eight feet high. Take the side poles and put them over the top of the front and back poles and lash them together. Cut four poles to stand up on the underside of the four support poles. Lash these to the center of the trees. This way they cannot work down the tree. Try to cut the top ends of these poles in an approximate 45 degree angle so the support poles sit in a notch and against the tree and cannot fall off.

Photo 4B

Tie one single cord around the middle to hold these poles in place against the tree. Add a center support on the walls and top support poles. We put a second pole about a foot under the front roof support pole so we can attach a piece of plastic on the front as a rain fly. Now you are ready to put on the roof poles. Place three or four poles on top of the back roof support poles toward the front roof support poles. Tie them tightly at each end so they cannot slide back and forth. Put a few the opposite way and just tie them loosely. These poles must be fairly light as we do not want to make the roof too heavy. The framework is now complete. It is time to unroll the plastic and begin to put the wall skin on.

Photo 4C

The plastic will be 25 feet long and 10 feet wide. Get the staple gun, hold the plastic sideways, and start stapling at the left corner. Put the plastic up to the top rail, leaving about two feet draped on the ground. There will be about four feet of the plastic left over at the back of the shelter as it is two feet shorter than the front. Staple it along the top a few times until you get to the back corner. Take the cardboard strips, hold them up against the poles, and staple about every three

Photo 4D

inches. At two-foot long intervals, go all the way across the top rail. Continue this spacing around the back until you run out of plastic. Now staple the cardboard strips to the plastic in the middle on the wall poles but alternate the cardboard stapling opposite of what you did on the top rail. Cut a six foot piece of plastic from the end of the other roll. Staple it on the last side to complete the wall framework. Find some short poles and rocks and lay them on the loose extra length of plastic all the way around to hold it in place. You should have a 19 foot x 10 foot piece of plastic left over. This will become the roof. Starting at the back, work the plastic up and over the top of the roof. From the inside you can take a small stick and move the plastic gently towards the front. Arrange it so it laps over all four tops of the walls. Staple and tie it the best you can. If you have some duct tape, you can tape it here and there. Using thin, long poles, throw them on top of the roof plastic to hold the plastic down when the wind blows. Try not to poke any holes in the roof plastic. If a hole does occur, you

Photo 4E

Comfortable camps like this are a necessity.

may patch it with duct tape. Your shelter is now completed. You should be planning for more than a weekend stay before constructing this type of shelter.

B. POTTY ROOMS

Look for a place downwind from camp. Try to pick a spot that is reasonably close to camp and that can be walked to in the dark with the aid of a flashlight, but will still allow for a good amount of privacy.

The first thing you will need is a toilet seat. A plywood cover works well with a toilet seat attached to the top. Using black plastic and some clear plastic for the top, you can construct an adequate potty room. Studying pictures 4-G and 4-H will assist you in the construction. Picture 4-H shows the doorway with a piece of black plastic pulled in front for privacy. Picture 4-I shows two logs stretched across two other logs about 1 1/2 feet in diameter. Place a piece of plastic in the front of the seat to guard your legs from any splattering.

Make sure you have room to stand in front of the seat with the door flap closed. Place a roll of toilet paper in a coffee can and seal it with the plastic lid. Pop holes in a mayonnaise jar lid with an ice pick, from the inside. Mix 75% lime with 25% carpet deodorizer. Fill the jar 3/4 full. Store the rest in a coffee can to refill the jar when empty. Sprinkle some lime mixture in the hole prior to using. To keep the jar from filling with rain water, cover it with plastic and a rubber band. After each use of the facility, shake the lime mix over the waste.

This lime mixture will eat up the waste and the carpet deodorant will make your potty room smell good. You will also notice very few flies around even if you use the facility for a very long time. Rake the floor of your potty room so you won't stumble in the dark. Some potty rooms can be 25 to 35 yards downwind through some tree cover from your gathering area. You might want to take some bathroom spray cleaner to disinfect the toilet seat. When you leave for home,

Photo 4G

take the potty room down, fill the hole and try to leave the area the way it was when you arrived. Also, it may be a good idea to check with the Forest Service regarding this type of facility before you start building it.

C. CHANGING BOOTHS

A good changing booth will be a 6 foot by 6 foot square. Make the booth at least 25 yards from camp for privacy and odor free clothes. You need not use large trees for construction of the changing booth. Note the sides are not over 5 feet high, the door is made the same way as the potty room door. Attach a pole from one tree to another inside the enclosure to make a place to hang your clothes. We use wire coat hangers so it looks like a closet. When hanging camo, be sure to have all your accessories; underwear, hat, socks, etc., with each set of camo. Allowing air circulation around your clothes will insure odor to dissipate as your camo hangs. (See

Photo 4H

picture 4-L.)

Remember deer can detect any trace of odor that is not natural. As you leave camp, leave your street clothes in the booth. When you return, change back into your street clothes. Placing a piece of plastic over the clothes will keep the dew off at night and in the morning. This booth is easy to assemble and will make a great difference in your success on scouting and hunting as you will eliminate more than 50% of the camp odors that spoil so many of the hunters' chances during their hunts.

Do not believe people who tell you that smoke from a fire will not spook a deer. Stop and think for a second. If you were a creature and smelled smoke, what would that mean to you? It would mean — where there is smoke there is fire! You probably would not take off running, but you would not go towards that scent. If the deer is looking your direction for whatever reason, most of the time the game of hunting him is over. The deer's eyes will fail him and his ears will fail him

Photo 4I

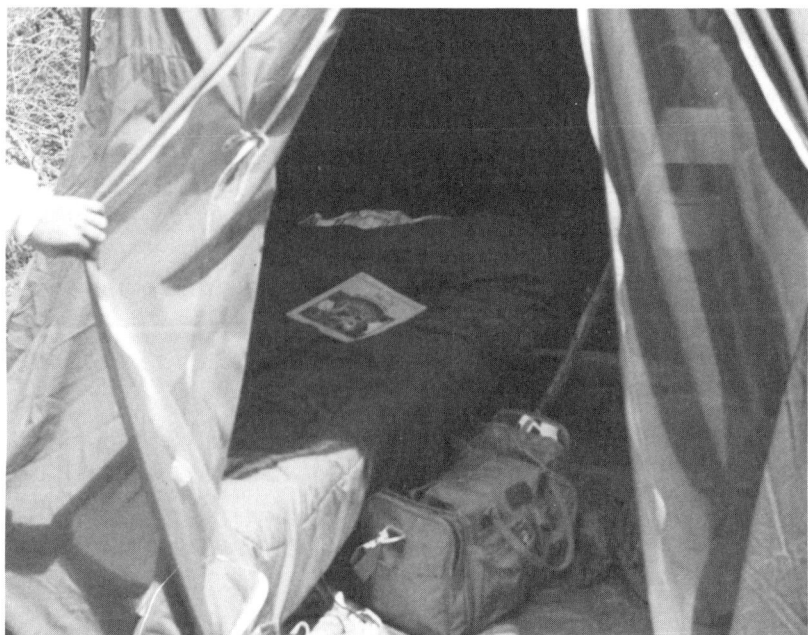

Photo 4J

sometimes but his nose only reports what it smells and when in doubt about danger, he will choose the message his nose relates every time.

D. TENT SELECTION

There are a number of tents on the market today. Whenever you look at tents, if they say they are a two-man tent, they are really a one-man tent. The reason we say this is you will need space to store your gear if you are going to backpack. The Boy Scout tent is a good choice. It is light and can be carried individually by people backpacking. Our tent selection will concentrate on tents that would be used in the early bow season and the first week of rifle season. Any other time we suggest you consult a person who has been at the area at the time of year you are planning to go or you may ask some local people near the area where you are scouting what the weather is like at that time of year. Using this information you should be able to make the correct tent choice.

For large parties, you have a choice of the canvas square tent or the large dome style tent. Or for the extra large parties, the very large wall tent is avaliable. The old-fashioned square tent is heavy to carry and so is the larger wall tent. These types should be used in a drive-in type camp. If your tent is not waterproof and there is a threat of rain, use a piece of plastic draped over it to accomplish waterproofing. Most tents you purchase today have a floor in them. We prefer not to use tents without floors, as a floor aids you in keeping critters out of your food and you may walk around inside your tent without shoes. Tired feet will be glad for this.

If you look at pictures 4-J and 4-K you will see one of our sleeping tents. This is a two-person tent. On each side you can see that the person's gear is stored under his cot. You will also notice a battery light hanging from a tripod made from three poles. Try to make your sleeping tent as comfortable as possible. It will make for better rest and you will be able to hunt harder and longer the next day. After your trip is over and you start to take your tent down, be sure to sweep out any debris from inside the tent as this material will cause holes and will sometimes cause the tent to rot. If the tent is wet and you cannot dry it before you pack it away, be sure to unfold it at home and dry it there. A piece of plastic laid down on the ground before you set up your tent will make it much easier to clean.

E. TYPES OF OUTDOOR COOKING

When you are backpacking on a weekend, the firepit is the best choice for cooking. All you will need is a metal grate. It can be an old refrigerator or freezer rack or an old barbecue grill as long as the grill is at least 2 foot by 2 foot square. The best shape for your pit should be like a keyhole. The smaller elongated part is the section for your cooking area. Either pile the dirt on the sides or line the sides with rocks. On picture 4-

Photo 4K

M you will see a space open at the end. This is so you can rake coals from the main fire into and under the grill. You can make a coal rake out of an old garden rake. With a hacksaw you can cut the ends off so there are only six inches or so of the rake attached to the handle.

You will also see at the bottom of the picture how to extend the handles on your pots and pans using old broom handles. Be sure to shape the end so it fits firmly on the pan or pot. A good fit is a must. Do not make the handles too long or the pans will not sit up.

Your last choice for cooking is the woodstove. Picture 4-N is a drawing showing a folding woodstove. After assembling the stove, you can attach a water can made from a *new* gas can along the side. Attach a metal spigot through the filling cap and this allows you to drain water when it is hot. This way you will always have hot water for camp chores. With this type of stove you will need some dirt placed in the

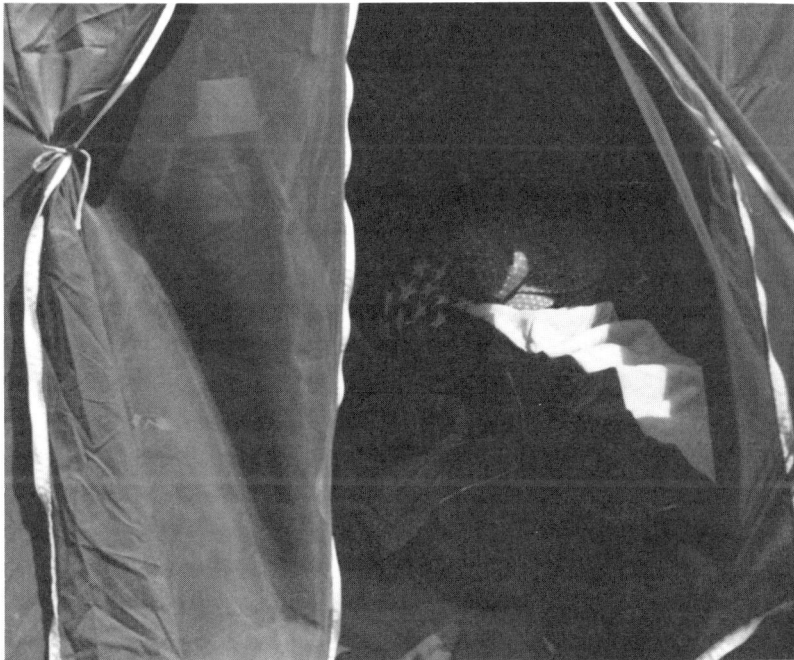

Photo 4L

bottom where the fire sits or the fire will burn through the bottom of the stove. You may be able to get more information from Safeport Manufacturing Co., Denver, CO 80211. The model we use is called the Sheepherders Model and sells for just under $100.00. This type of stove is perfect during the times when open wood fires are not permitted which happens frequently during the early bow season. The stovepipes are not included with the stove. You can use a six inch clothes dryer pipe which is light and inexpensive but will need to be replaced frequently. A small barbecue grill with a lid works well for some kinds of cooking. It is important to have a lid for quick cooking for chicken and other thick items as without it they will not cook all the way through in a short period of time.

No matter which cooking and heating method you decide to use, be sure to be careful when cooking as fire destroys much timber each year. The larger your party the larger your cooking method has to be. Using these methods, your food will always taste better cooked outdoors for some reason or another.

As you are aware, small critters can be very destructive to a camp while you are away. So be sure to keep all food inside your tent and sealed up.

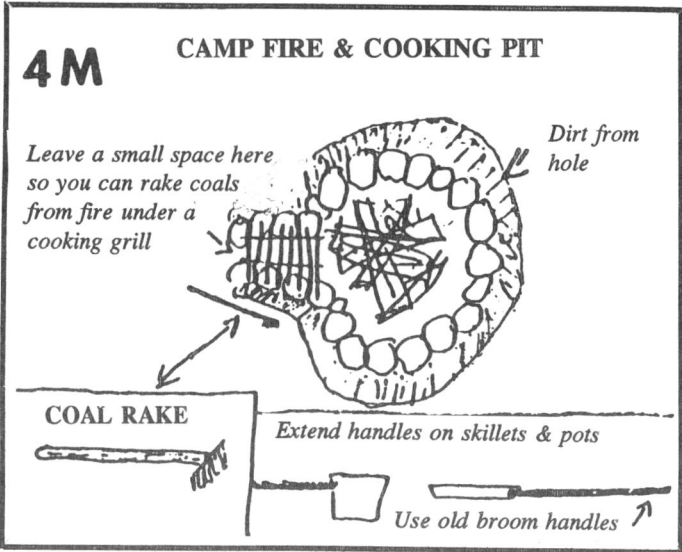

4 M   CAMP FIRE & COOKING PIT

Leave a small space here so you can rake coals from fire under a cooking grill

Dirt from hole

COAL RAKE

Extend handles on skillets & pots

Use old broom handles

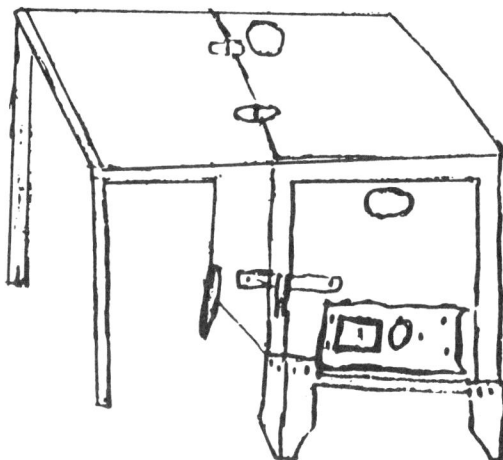

FOLDING CAMP STOVE

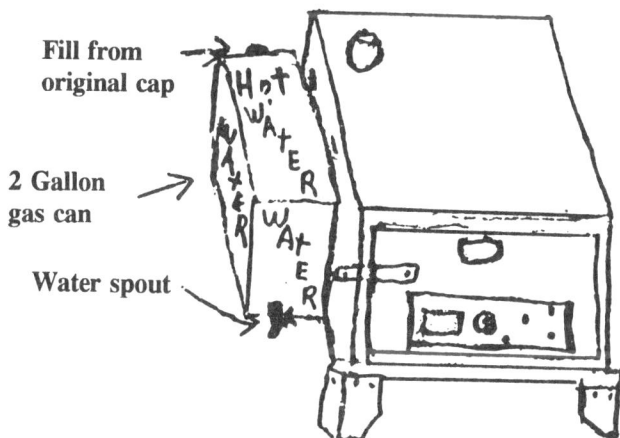

Fill from
original cap

H o t
W a t e r

W a t e r

2 Gallon
gas can

W A t e r

Water spout

Illustration 4N

A blacktail buck in the fall.

CHAPTER 5

COOKING RECIPES

A. HOME PREPARATION

Depending on the length of the trip, you can prepare many menus ahead of time at home to make cooking at camp easier and quicker. Even though you plan for three meals a day you might only use two or as many as four a day. This will depend on what you are doing each day. If you are backpacking without a refrigerator or ice box, you are limited to what you can take. Most beginners depend on freeze dried foods. If you use these types of foods, you will need to eat much fiber and drink much water. Without the fiber you will more than likely develop diarrhea.

When packaging your staples, try to pack most of them in plastic bags. The Ziploc kind work great but other kinds will work if you can seal them from leaking. Planning your meals will prevent you from packing more food than you need on your trip. Make a list and use it to determine how many staples to package and how many packages you will need. This can also keep your costs down considerably. The freeze dried food we have tried tastes very bland. Here is a list of staples used when we go camping: sugar, salt, pepper, catsup, mustard, mayonnaise packets, honey, jelly, creamer, and even crackers. None of these need refrigeration. Be sure that you can prepare your choice of food under primitive cooking conditions and with the type stove or fire you have chosen to use. When backpacking, determine how many people are in your party and how many days your stay will be. Drinks in single serving mixtures are the best for dispensing. Salt and pepper are our basic seasonings. Saltine or other crackers are a necessity to prevent diarrhea. Dried spaghetti sauce, gravy mixes or any food mixes that do not need refrigeration are items that could be used for camp cooking. Unpopped popcorn is another good choice. It can be popped in a skillet over any kind of heat. We use vegetable shortening, as in this solid form it cannot spill while being transported. For cleaning pots and pans we use scouring pads, as most of the time you will burn some food because you will have trouble regulating the heat on the fire.

B. BARBECUING FOODS

If you plan to cook fish, chicken, steaks, hamburger or other meats, they should be frozen to help them stay cold for as long as possible. Keeping them packed on ice in an ice box also keeps them frozen until it's time to use them. Flour, cornmeal or any baking mix is the only other item we use on a regular basis. As we said before, try all sauces, gravy mixes, etc., at home to make sure it is to your taste. Any barbecue coals will work fine as long as they have not drawn moisture. Vegetables are the most difficult items to cook while camping. We make hobo vegetables. You may use any kind of vegetables — potatoes, celery, carrots, corn, broccoli, onions or cauliflower. Be sure to add two pats of butter or margarine, place single servings in a piece of aluminum foil, season to your taste and close the top. Place on the grill. Turn them several times and in about 10 to 20 minutes they are ready. In our experiences this has been the easiest way to prepare vegetables. Corn on the cob can be cooked on fire coals or barbecue grill in the husk — silkhairs and all. Turn them often and in about 20 to 30 minutes, depending on the heat, they will be ready. When cooking steaks or hamburger we prefer thicker ones than you would use at home, as barbecuing tends to dry out meat when it cooks. Most people tend to overcook items under primitive cooking methods. Remember you can always put it back on the fire if it is undercooked but you will have to eat it if it is overcooked.

C. COOKING LIVER AND RIBS

Deer liver cannot be kept for very long without being cool. We usually eat the liver within 24 hours of the time we get it. Here are some ways you can prepare the liver.

Soak the liver in salt water overnight, then peel and slice it. Take 2 tsp. of butter, 1/2 cup of salt pork, one large onion (minced), 1/2 tsp. of seasoning, 1 lemon (peeled), 1/2 cup of chopped cooked bacon and 2 eggs. Place butter, liver, salt pork and onions in a large skillet. Cook at low heat until tender. Soak 3 slices of bread in 1 cup of milk, mix seasoning, bacon and eggs and pour over the entire mixture. Cook at low heat for 1 1/2 hours or until tender. Serve with toast to complete the meal.

Another recipe for liver is to soak the liver in salt water overnight, skin and slice in thick slices. Chop six onions. Saute the onions in a large skillet. Fill a plastic bag with 1 cup of flour and seasoning to your taste. Shake one slice of liver at a time in the mixture. Cook with the onions at low heat for about 15 minutes, then add more onions and cook until done.

Another food difficult to cook is ribs. We do not pack bones so we eat ribs in camp. We are sure our recipes for ribs will be a hit in your camp.

Melt one stick of butter, add two tsp. of oil. Mix 1/3 cup of vinegar and 4 tsp. of worchestershire sauce. Brown the ribs on the grill, then chop them into small pieces and place in a pan. Pour sauce ingredients over ribs and cook slowly for 2 hours or until tender. Sprinkle with brown sugar and serve hot.

Another way we like to eat ribs is to prepare 3 cups of

rice per package directions. Chop ribs into 3 inch by 3 inch pieces. Mix 1/2 cup tomato sauce and a small amount of water with a package of dried spaghetti sauce mix. Simmer until hot, then add over the ribs. Cook until meat is tender. Serve over the top of the rice. You may also add some peas to this mixture for a complete meal. This will make 6 servings.

D. SIMPLE MENUS

When hunting or scouting, your meals need to be simple to prepare but nutritious. Beforehand you should decide whether each person is going to cook for themselves or if someone is the designated camp cook. If you have picky eaters in your party we suggest that everyone do his own cooking. Remember, not everyone comes back to camp at the same time and not everyone is hungry at the same time, so trying to keep food warm under these conditions is very difficult.

Some people are not breakfast eaters. We like eating breakfast at around 11 a.m. after we return from sitting in our tree stands all morning. Some people cannot go without breakfast. In large parties this problem is common. We do eat doughnuts, toast or rolls with our coffee, tea, cocoa or spiced cider in the mornings.

E. ALL-TIME FAVORITE VENISON MEALS

After eating venison for 40 years we have assembled some of our favorite recipes to help you enjoy your deer meat year after year. Any recipe that calls for red meat can be altered to suit deer meat. We have never had a bad piece of deer meat we have taken care of ourselves. If someone is trying to pawn off LARGE amounts of deer meat there is usually something wrong with it. We hope these recipes will help you enjoy a change of pace rather than the plain old deer steaks and deer roasts.

NO. 1 DUTCH OVEN VENISON

5 pounds of boned venison chunks
1 1/2 pounds of sauerkraut
8 small potatoes, 8 carrots and onions
1/2 cup vinegar, 2/3 cups of water
1/2 cup oil
garlic, onion powder, your choice of seasoning
      Place oil and 5 pounds of boned venison in a dutch oven and coat it with the seasoning, garlic and onion powder. Brown meat on all sides, add the vinegar and water, roll the meat over to coat all sides. Place it on medium heat for about 15 minutes. Add potatoes, carrots and onions. Allow it to cook for another 20 minutes. Heat sauerkraut and add to the pot. Place back on heat 45 minutes to 1 hour. It is ready to enjoy.

NO. 2 MARINATED STEAKS

1 venison steak per person
1 cup of A-1 sauce
1/2 cup of catsup
2 chopped onions
Your choice of seasoning
2 potatoes per person
      Combine A-1 sauce, catsup and seasoning in a large bowl. Pound steaks slightly and marinate steaks for 3 hours. In hot oil, sear the steaks on both sides. Remove them and add sliced onions and sliced potatoes to the skillet. Brown this mixture. Place the steaks in the skillet and simmer at low heat until steaks are a little rare. Remember venison becomes dry if it is overcooked. There should be just a trace of red color in the center when steaks are done.

NO. 3 VENISON STEW

2 or 3 pounds of venison chunks
4 chopped carrots, 4 potatoes and onions
1/2 cup of celery, 1/2 green pepper
1 can of red or kidney beans
2 cups of water
1/2 cup parsley, your choice of seasoning
1 cup red wine
     Brown stew meat in a small amount of oil in a large pot. Add all ingredients at once to the pot and bring the mixture to a boil. Reduce heat to simmer. Cook at this temperature for 4 to 6 hours. Remember the more you simmer stew the thicker it becomes. Stir the stew often so it cooks evenly.

NO. 4 BEER BATTER VENISON STEAKS

1 steak per person
12 oz. beer
1 package batter mix
1 cup lemon juice
1 cup flour
Oil
1 box of rice mix, your choice
     Pound the venison steaks and preheat a skillet with oil. Mix the batter per instructions on the package, but use the beer in place of water. Dip steaks into lemon juice, then in the flour and in the batter mix. Fry until meat is done to your taste. Prepare rice and add to the steaks to make a complete meal.

NO. 5 VENISON STRIPS AND NOODLES

1 venison steak per person
1 box of noodles
1/2 cup of wine
2 cloves of garlic

1 - 8 oz. can of tomato sauce
1 pat of butter
Your choice of seasoning

Prepare noodles per instructions on the box. Cut venison into strips. In a skillet, saute the venison in the wine for 5 minutes. Add the can of tomato sauce and crush in garlic and butter. Simmer until meat is done. Spoon meat on top of the noodles, adding all the sauce.

NO. 6 HORSERADISH MEAT DIP

2 bottles of chutney
5 tsp. of horseradish
1 tsp. of wine.

Cook venison to desired taste. Mix the ingredients above and dip.

NO. 7 VENISON POT PIE

2 pounds of venison
1 can of peas
1 can of diced carrots
1/2 cup of raisins
2 potatoes, diced
1 box of biscuit dough mix

Cut venison into chunks. Brown the venison in the oven. In a separate pot, empty 1 can of peas, not drained, and 1 can of diced carrots, 1/2 cup of raisins. Dice potatoes small and cook for 15 minutes at medium heat. Add the meat. Place all this in a dish, cover ingredients with the biscuit dough (per recipe on box). Place in the oven for 15 to 25 minutes at 400 degrees. Serve hot from the oven.

NO. 8 VENISON HASH

2 pounds of venison
2 lbs. of peeled potatoes, cut in cubes

1 package of gravy mix
1 pound of chopped mushrooms
1/2 tsp. of garlic powder
1/2 tsp. of pepper
1/8 tsp. of basil

Cube venison and cut potatoes into a skillet. Heat and mix gravy with the meat. Simmer for 20 minutes. Add mushrooms and simmer for 15 more minutes. Add the rest of the ingredients and stir. Heat for another 15 minutes or until meat is done. Serve on toast with an egg if desired.

NO. 9 MEXICAN VENISON CHILI

3 pounds of venison
1 bell pepper (chopped)
2 cloves of garlic (crushed)
3 tsp. of chili powder
1 - 2 Tbls. of hot pepper
2 - 15 oz. cans of kidney beans
1 quart of water
1 tsp. of paprika
1 medium onion diced

Brown venison in a large pot. Remove venison from pot. Saute onions and bell peppers. Add spices to taste. Add meat and kidney beans to the large pot. Add 2 cups of water. Reheat and add all the remaining ingredients. Simmer for 3 to 5 hours, stirring occasionally. Add more water if needed. That's all there is to it.

NO. 10 VENISON CORDON BLEU

2 steaks per person (beat until thin)
16 ozs. of cheese (any kind)
2 Tbl. parsley, 1 egg, 1/4 cup milk
1/2 cup chopped onions

Salt and pepper
1 tsp. of ginger
1 cup bread crumbs

Mix cheese, onions, parsley, salt, pepper and ginger in a bowl. Place a small amount of mixture in the middle of each steak. Fold in ends and roll up steaks. Use a toothpick to secure them. Roll meat in flour, egg and milk mixture then in bread crumbs. Brown in butter in a skillet. Place in a baking dish lined with aluminum foil. Cover with another piece of foil. Bake for 30 to 45 minutes at 350 degrees. Serve with small red parslied potatoes or steamed vegetables and rice.

NO. 11 VENISON FAJITAS

2 lbs. venison, sliced in thin strips
1 tsp. of ginger
2 peeled onions, cut in half and sliced
3 green peppers, chopped
A small amount of oil
Taco sauce
Tortillas (flour)
Onion powder
1 cup of tomatoes (chopped)

Sprinkle meat on both sides with ginger, garlic and some onion powder. Cook meat until done. Remove venison and place in aluminum foil. In the same skillet, cook sliced onions. Place meat, then onions, green peppers and tomatoes with taco sauce inside warmed flour tortilla. Serve with a salad.

NO. 12 BURRITOS WITH VENISON

1 1/2 pounds of venison stew meat
2 medium potatoes (peeled and cubed)
1 onion, chopped fine
2 cups water
2 beef boullion cubes

1 clove of garlic, crushed
Ginger and seasoning to taste
1 package of gravy mix
12 inch (flour) tortillas

Sprinkle venison with ginger and seasoning. In a pressure cooker, brown onions, garlic and meat together. Add water and boullion cubes, cover. After cooker comes up to pressure, cook ingredients for 15 minutes. Cool pressure cooker per instructions. Add gravy mix. Thicken mixture with corn starch if necessary. Heat tortillas. Dish out the mixture in the middle of the tortillas. If you desire, add some taco sauce, lettuce, tomatoes, chopped onions and serve with corn chips.

NO. 13 TANGY VENISON CHILI

1 1/2 lbs. venison stew meat
2 cloves of garlic (crushed)
1 medium onion (diced)
2 Tbl. of oil
Salt and Pepper
1 small green pepper
1 can of kidney beans
1 can of corn
1/4 cup of taco sauce
1 can of stewed tomatoes
1 Tbl. chili powder

Put two tablespoons of oil in a pot. Heat the oil and place the venison, onion, green pepper and garlic in. Salt and pepper to taste. Cook ingredients until onions are soft and meat is browned. Add chili powder, stewed tomatoes, kidney beans with the juice, corn and taco sauce. Serve with corn bread or saltine crackers. This tastes even better the next day!

NO. 14 STROGANOFF VENISON

1 cup water
1 boullion cube

1 1/2 pounds of venison stew meat
2 onions (chopped)
2 cloves of garlic (crushed)
2 Tbl. of oil
1 cup of sour cream
Noodles or rice

Salt and pepper venison to taste. Place onions and garlic in a pot with heated oil and cook until golden brown. Remove from pot. Add meat to pot, then brown. Replace onion, garlic mixture and add water and boullion cube. Adjust heat to low. Cook until water is almost gone. Remove from heat and add sour cream. Serve over noodles or rice.

NO. 15 ROULADEN VENISON

1 steak per person
Salt and pepper
2 Tbl. chopped onion for each steak
1/2 cup of water
1 small pickle per steak (chopped)
1 boullion cube (dissolved)
Flour and oil
Mustard (your choice)

Pound steaks until thin. Salt and pepper. Spread one side of the steaks with mustard. Add chopped onions and pickles on top of each steak. Roll up steaks and secure with a toothpick. Roll in flour and brown in hot oil on all sides. Add 1/2 cup of water and boullion cube. Cover and cook at medium heat until water is evaporated. Serve with either fried potatoes or German potato salad.

We hope these ideas will help you enjoy venison as much as we do. Keep in mind that just about any beef meat recipe can be made with venison. So experiment a little and enjoy your venison more.

Jim with a 28-inch 5x5 mule deer buck taken with the bow at 18 yards.

Wes with a 23-inch 3x5 mule deer taken with the bow at 40 yards.

CHAPTER 6

EARLY OR LATE SEASON HUNTING

A. WARM WEATHER HUNTING

Our favorite time to hunt is during warm weather. One advantage to hunting this time of year is that you are the first hunters in the woods. The deer are relaxed and have a sense of security. They have seen many fishermen and have less fear of man at this time of year. Another big plus to hunting at this time is the buck's antlers are still in velvet. At this time the antlers are very tender so most bucks walk in and alongside the clearings, picking the less brushy terrain to move through. After their antlers have hardened, usually during rifle season, you will not be able to force them out of the thick brush.

Bucks have a high demand for nutrition during this early season. One reason is to supply their growing antlers with the large quantity of calcium needed to produce a large set of antlers. As the buck seeks the best feeding areas he tends to feed longer, gorging himself more than he would during any other time in the summer. After a hard winter the buck is also trying to put on the needed fat that will aid him during the rut and the coming winter.

At this time he is running in small bachelor groups. From two to as many as twenty bucks may be seen in one bunch. The only disadvantage to seeing more than one buck at a time is that there are too many opportunities for one of the bucks to be alerted to your presence. However, this will also allow you to size up the buck's antlers compared to others and see more deer in a smaller area.

With knowledge we will give you in the coming chapters, combined with long sunny days and clear nights, you will be able to predict deer movement. You need to study the moon. Depending if the moon is full, dark, or even in between, you need to understand how to use the moon to your advantage. This time is critical because more deer are out at night. Full moonlit nights help the deer see better in the dark. Even though they have good night vision, it seems that more deer will feed quicker under these moonlighted conditions.

In our opinion, you will see fewer deer at daylight after a full moonlit night than you will after a dark night. We prefer to scout for deer during the full moonlit nights. The reason is that the deer can be seen much better in the clearings right after it becomes dark. The deer tend to come down from their bedding areas and start feeding sooner than they do on a dark night. While scouting in the late evening your sight is also better and you can compare antler size easier than you can if it is too dark. The purpose of scouting both daylight and dark is to determine whether your tree stand placement will be more effective in morning or the afternoon hunt. Although we prefer to hunt deer on days after the non-moonlit nights, as they tend to be out longer just after dawn, most hunters are aware that daylight is the best time of day to harvest a buck. As the long warm days drag on, the deer will tend to water more frequently. Sometimes they will even water in the middle of the day.

Deer see fishermen frequently and hunters and campers occasionally. During most of the summer the deer will tolerate a certain amount of commotion close to their living area. Have you ever heard the joke about the deer saying, "Run, the red-hat army is here." That has much truth to it when there is an increase of human activity, such as during rifle season. Smart bucks notice vehicle traffic the night before the season opens.

Deer are out at night and will notice the slightest difference in patterns. The oldest bucks have seen a few hunting seasons and will fade out of sight and probably not be seen for the rest of the season. Spikes and forkies are not as aware of what is going on. If the small buck is lucky enough to be with an older buck, he might slide away himself even though he doesn't know why. If you happen to run onto these bucks, the older buck will use the inexperienced buck as a

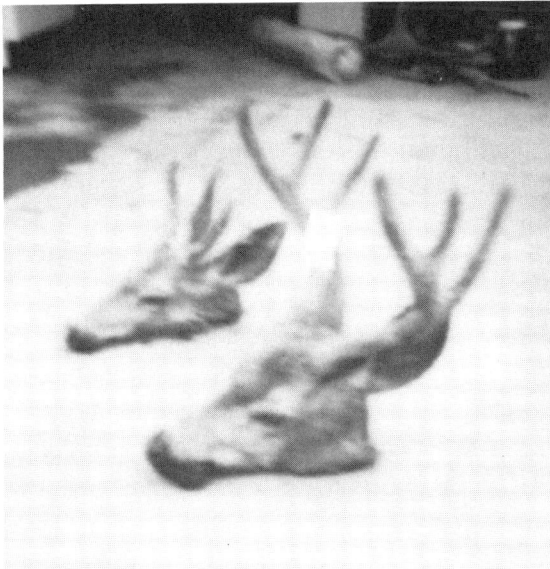

Photo 6A

blocker between you and him. These small bucks, unfortunately, are not around very long as they are usually in the stew pot. In picture 6-A you will see two bucks we harvested in one season. The three-point was taken on the first morning, but as the hunt continued, we had to settle for a spike buck as all the other large bucks we saw during our scouting days showed indications that they were aware of the hunt. Never underestimate the deer's ability to be alerted when something is different than normal. Another factor that persuades us to hunt the early bow season is that most children are out of school. Hunting the first week will allow the family to go without having to take the children out of school. In Oregon the archery season is the last week of August and the children resume school after the Labor Day weekend.

If you plan fishing activities during this period the fishing normally is still good and gives the smaller children something to do during the day.

Most of the bucks, such as the ones shown in picture 6-B, were aware of human activity around them. During this season, about three or four years ago, there were two poor fawn survival rates in a row. Knowing this, we made up our minds to take the first forkies or larger bucks we saw. That is what we harvested — two forkies and one three point.

As most of our hunting party does not like to hunt in wet brush, we chose to hunt the early season so as to assure most of our hunting days would be dry. We, as hunters, know if a deer is hit with either a gun or bow and it is raining, or begins to rain shortly after the hit, the blood trail will be washed away.

Ninety percent of all deer shot under these conditions will be lost. A true sportsman considers this — a lost deer is the most sickening circumstance that could happen to him. Not hunting in the rain will assure you, most of the time, of finding your animal's blood trail. To avoid this problem, watch the sky and smell the air. Most of the time the direction the wind is blowing is the direction the weather comes from. It should not be difficult to determine what the next hours will bring weatherwise.

What do you do on rainy days? You may sleep, catch up on camp chores or maybe fish between showers. Remember, it is quite miserable to sit in a tree stand during bad weather and deer do not feed much during rain storms. Normally, they seek thick cover to stand or lay in, trying to keep as dry as possible. The first thunder and lightning storm I was in was in 1989 during archery deer season. I will tell you what we observed.

The storm came late in the afternoon. By evening the lightning flashed so bright that it looked like daylight in the

Photo 6B

tents. Our dog was so frightened she was trying to dig a hole in the floor. The thunder boomed like a cannon. This continued until 1:00 a.m. If the storm had lasted longer, we would have stayed in camp that day. But as we arose, the sky was somewhat clear. We hadn't hunted after such a storm before. We prepared to hunt as we would any other time. After returning to camp, our reports were — no kills or sightings that morning. We are aware now, that after such a storm you are better off sleeping in. The deer were holding tight in the thickest cover they could find. The next morning we were up early and pondered what the day would bring. I personally saw one of the biggest bucks I had ever seen in the past five years. My attempt to shoot him was fruitless as I could not concentrate on arrow placement. My eyes kept moving towards his head, surveying the massive antlers. My shot was low and I still have dreams of that day.

My son did great! He harvested the biggest buck of his hunting career and the biggest one our entire party took that hunting season. My dad was like me. As he drew on his four-pointer and looked through the peep sight, he saw the gray body. He let the arrow go and heard a thud. He saw his buck running away but his arrow was nowhere to be seen. As he looked around, he saw his arrow shaking in a large gray log. He did hit what he was aiming at, but it wasn't the deer.

There are fewer people in the woods in the early season and we believe most hunters are waiting for the last two weeks in order to get closer to the buck rut season when the buck is more careless. Mule deer do not rut until mid-November, well after the rifle season. As you can guess, we will never be able to hunt mule deer at that time because all of Oregon's mule deer seasons are finished by the first week of October.

B. COLD WEATHER HUNTING

There are some good reasons to hunt in cold weather. One reason is that after a few weeks of hunting, the deer begin to accept the fact that people are hunting them. They begin to set their patterns. As their antlers have hardened by now, you may notice more deer in thickets. Using this information, you may concentrate your hunting efforts in and around that type of terrain.

If you hunt blacktail in the late November season you may have an excellent chance to bag one of the "big boys." Picture 6-C shows a unique set of blacktail antlers I harvested on the late hunt during rifle season. The antlers protruded forward in an exaggerated manner. As I examined the antlers in the thick brush, I was sure he was a trophy class animal. After downing and retrieving him I discovered he was only a forkie — but what a forkie. Blacktails are hunted during the rut both in the general rifle season and the late bow season in Oregon. During the November season, most of the high terrain is snowed in. Snow does make for excellent tracking. If the snow depth is slightly over ten or twelve inches the deer will normally move to lower elevations leaving them more concentrated in foraging areas.

Most of the blacktail bucks, during the late season, are running with does or else totally by themselves. Having only one pair of eyes and one set of ears to warn them of dangers allows you to make stalks on the loners much easier.

When bucks are in herds, it is like trying to stalk a flock of geese — one is always looking. Another advantage to hunting the late season is, if you have done much hunting, you will be aware of where and how the deer are traveling. This should allow you to be in the right place at the right time more

Photo 6C

often than you were in the early season.

In the late season you don't have the problem with warm temperatures that will spoil your deer meat if it is not recovered in a reasonable amount of time. You also do not have problems with blow flies, bees and hornets attacking you and the carcass while you are trying to butcher. If you are looking for a good head mount, the late season bucks have better looking capes than the summer ones. The thick winter gray coats seem more natural than the long reddish hair found on the deer in the early hunting season. Late season blacktail have antlers that are dark and rich looking. During the early season the antlers are usually in velvet or are starting to peel, exposing the bone-white antlers that look ragged. Most people don't associate this type of antler with the normal mounted bucks they've seen.

Rattling and grunting for blacktail deer is best accomplished in the very last weeks of the season. Picture 6-D shows another fine blacktail forkie harvested while using a small amount of rattling and grunting during the last week of the season.

A final advantage to hunting the end of the season is that many hunters have given up or have their deer. Some have run out of funds for hunting or the weather is so severe they would rather sit in front of the fire at home. This tends to make fewer hunters and will make the bucks less wary. Hopefully, the bucks will drop their guard and you will have an opportunity to harvest a trophy class deer.

Photo 6D

CHAPTER 7

MULE DEER HABITS AND HABITAT

A. STUDYING MULE DEER MOVEMENT

Mule deer move both day and night, but feel safest under the cover of darkness with a full moon. A full moon you say! Under cover of a full moon doesn't cover the deer's movement much — and you are right. You must understand that at night with no moon the deer do see better than you do. However, they do not move as well without the moonlight.

During our observations we discovered places where deer prefer to move under the cover of darkness. We concentrated our research for a two-week period in three areas. One of the places we call "the foot." It is a small hillside with little gullies running up and down. This area is only 1,000 yards across and the rolling hills drop down into a large meadow and swamp. The deer living in this area of the canyon spend the day on the slopes of the hill, resting in large groves of green-leafed manzanita. The manzanita is so dense in these places that in order for a person to get through, he must walk on and through the tangled growth. The brush is higher than your head in some places. Even trying to pick your way through in a zig-zag manner will be too noisy to attempt an approach on a deer.

With one person in a tree stand recording everything he could see or hear, we studied the behavior of each deer we saw. Some days were sunny, hot, calm days. Others were cloudy, cool and windy days. The observer in the tree stand would signal uphill to tell the other person the direction of the deer. This person would try to move as close to the deer as he could.

Recording the movement of the deer as soon as it showed any awareness of the stalker, we determined deer hear you coming and can avoid you easily.

The first day my son and father watched as I tried to stalk two deer. My father and son had a good view of the two deer moving uphill to a bedding site. They watched and recorded the results as the two deer were moving up from the swamp where they had fed and watered the night before.

The first deer was a large, non-typical five or six point. It was difficult even with 8x25 binoculars to see all of his small tines on the spreading and twisted antlers. The second deer was a fair-antlered three-point. Most deer are grayish in color, just as the smaller three-point deer looked, but the significant difference was that the big buck was as black as a stove.

A biologist told us later that the black buck had been seen before when he was a yearling. This buck returns to this general area each year. The biologist told us the frequency of a black deer is one out of 200,000 deer born, compared to an albino deer, which is one out of every 100,000. This makes our sighting of the black deer a once in a lifetime occurrence.

We sat for more than three hours watching and recording the movement of these two deer. After they had bedded for about one hour, we decided to begin our experiment. After studying the terrain, I decided to work my way down the right side of the clearing. When I was even with the deer, my father and son would give me the signal to start moving toward the deer. I moved as slowly as I could. There was no way to stay quiet due to the tangled, dry green-leafed manzanita cover. I sounded like a two-ton elephant charging through the brush. As I moved closer, the smaller buck, which was bedded below and about 25 yards to the right of the big black buck, was the first to hear me. The wind was swirling and he rose to his feet, raised his head and tested the wind with his nostrils and caught my scent. Then he lowered his head and almost crawled through the thick cover. He moved down and disappeared like an apparition fading away.

I was disoriented in this tangled mess. I stopped to check my father and son through my binoculars. With hand signals they told me the bucks were aware of me but that the large black buck was still bedded. With the smaller buck already moving, the black buck was searching with his ears and nose. Not wanting to rise in what he considered imminent danger, he held his spot. Not until he was sure of my location did he attempt his escape. I didn't get any closer than 45 yards and all I saw was the top of his rack moving downhill. Not running full out, but fast enough to give me no chance to make an attempt to shoot at him if I had been hunting. What we discovered was that these deer bed down in the morning sun, as many deer do. As the morning progresses and the temperature rises, they will move to a cooler and shadier spot.

If undisturbed, the mule deer will remain in that location until late afternoon or early evening. Mule deer will begin to move just after sunset. Much like us when we first get up, they will stretch, look, listen for a few minutes and then, like us, will meander to the "breakfast table" to drink and eat. Mule deer normally do not go far until it is completely dark to cover their ascent toward the feeding and watering area.

The anticipation to start down early is a mistake some deer make that you can use to your advantage. Some deer will peck at brush as they make their way down the hill. They are moving but not as fast as they do during the darkness. If you have watched deer in any area, you should be able to place your stand near a path where the mule deer are likely to pass.

If the buck leaves a little early, he will give you an excellent chance for a shot at him. Remember, if you place your stand too far downhill, the deer will not get to your location until it is too dark to shoot and if you are too close to the bedding grounds you will spook the deer when you try to get in and out of your stand.

Placement of your stand is critical, so study all the possible locations closely. Mule deer move somewhat fast toward water and feed just after dark. Normally, deer try to get a drink first, before seriously starting to feed. They feed for about 4 1/2 to 5 1/2 hours per night. Sometimes they get a second drink before starting back to their day beds. This second drink will, most of the time, give you that morning shot, as this delay will make the buck late getting to his bed. Most bucks are in their beds before daylight.

If a buck dawdles for any reason, he will be close to his bed but not in it at daylight. He will be within 50 to 100 yards short of the bed. This is where you should have your stand. Finding deer beds is one key to successfully harvesting a buck from a tree stand.

At this time we need to let you know what a buck deer does in a 24-hour period. Deer have 8 hours of darkness in which to travel, feed and water before returning to their beds before daylight. Most deer, especially the older bucks, complete this task day after day. Within this time period, all deer make mistakes of one form or another.

You must be able to analyze your observations and decipher your notes on local deer to be able to harvest a buck. We know from our studies and research that the deer we hunt spend 4 1/2 to 5 1/2 hours feeding, leaving 3 to 3 1/2 hours to travel from their beds to feed and water and return to their beds before daylight each day.

These and other facts have brought us to a conclusion. A deer spends 1 1/2 to 1 3/4 hours traveling each way. This is an average time schedule. It could be as much as 4 1/2 or as little as 2 hours travel time depending on the distance and how steep the terrain is. Remember, you must do your own research in your area to be sure you know what, where and how the deer movement can be predicted. During full moonlit nights you can sit and observe deer feeding in most meadows. When you are observing deer, each person should pick a buck to watch, take notes, mark down the time the deer came into the clearing, from which direction, how the deer moved around in the clearing, feeding and watering, and which direction he left the clearing.

The next morning, approach the spot where the deer was seen last. Study the cover closely to see if there is a place where you can set up. In the afternoon, start where the buck left the clearing, begin walking up the hill, moving slowly. Try to stay near the main trails. The majority of tracks indicate the trail the deer are using. Do not walk directly on the trail or the deer will pick up your scent. Move slowly toward the deer beds. Do not try to rush. Mule deer are somewhat homebodies. If undisturbed, they will usually stay within a five mile square. Only during migration is this not true.

The farmland mule deer usually will stay in one place for most of their life. But, if disturbed, all mule deer will seek a more remote place to live. Try to hunt where there is little or no hunting pressure. Our statistics show that hunting disturbed deer is twice as difficult as hunting undisturbed deer. After sleeping all day, the deer start stirring again as the sun goes down and the whole process starts over again.

By studying drawing 7-A, you can visualize how deer move. Look at the key on the bottom of the drawing. Start at the deer beds in the mountain. This process is a 24-hour movement pattern of a typical mule deer's life. One problem you will have is finding your tree stand in the dark. To aid you in this endeavor, try purchasing some Game Tracker reflector tacks. You will find them in most bow hunting catalogs. Figure 7-B shows a Game Tracker reflector tack.

B. STUDYING MULE DEER HABITS

When you study the habits of local deer, be sure to

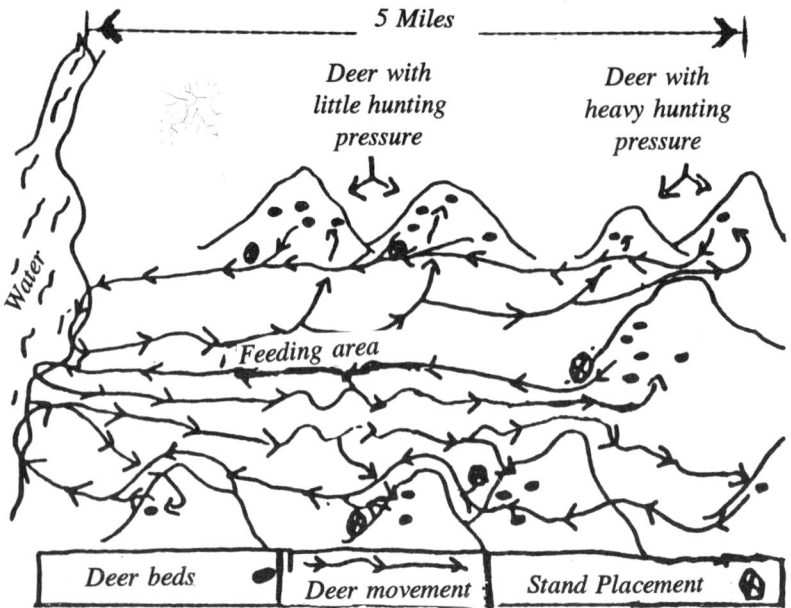

5 Miles

Deer with little hunting pressure

Deer with heavy hunting pressure

Water

Feeding area

| Deer beds | Deer movement | Stand Placement |

Illustration 7A

make notes as you can never remember all you have learned. However, deer habits are not carved in stone. Something as small as a change in the wind direction may spook a deer. But if you do not have the wind direction written down, how could you compare and study his reaction and movement to different wind conditions. Slowly you will analyze and come to the conclusion why the deer did what he did, comparing each day's notes to others from that year. The pattern changes and statistical differences or similarities are the best aids you can have to accomplish this.

Most devoted mule deer hunters I know spend much time studying as many hunting logs as they can get their hands on. They look for that common denominator which will allow them to predict mule deer habits. Logs are the biggest advantage a hunter can have over another hunter. It will usually mean the difference between harvesting a buck or seeing one running away from you.

C. TYPES OF MULE DEER TERRAIN

Mule deer may live near humans, as on farms, or as far away from humans as possible. As long as the deer have food, water and hiding shelter, they are satisified to live out their lives where they are feeling secure. When any of the survival items are gone, so are the deer.

Mule deer like easy living. Bucks, even big ones, seek out these places. Around farms is one of their favorite places, but getting permission to hunt these places is getting tougher each year. Any good mule deer terrain must have water. Without water there is very little hope that it will hold any deer. Good mule deer terrain will also have pole thickets for the deer to hide in and some of the terrain must have rolling hills for escape routes. A good supply of browse to feed on is the last necessary item the area must have to hold mule deer. Knowing what mule deer like to eat will make your search easier.

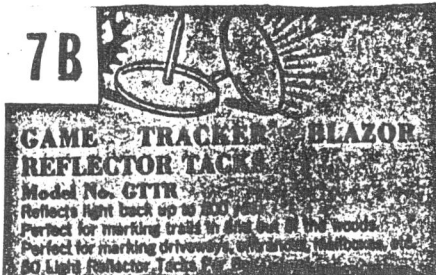

Illustration 7B

Figure 7-C shows the green-leafed manzanita the bucks love to hide in. Also shown are open areas deer use to move through when their antlers are in velvet. Mule deer bucks will avoid the heavier brush during the antler growing stages.

Figure 7-D shows a small forky in such a place. You can see the bitter brush they eat and small evergreens that help the bucks hide when they move from place to place. And, you can also see that his antlers are well out of the brush, preventing the sensitive antlers from being hit or rubbed as he moves around. Bucks will bunch up in bachelor groups and

Photo 7C

will travel inside a particular realm of their home terrain.

Deer must and will leave tracks. Where there are no tracks, or very few tracks, there are very few or no deer. Picutre 7-E shows a very well used deer trail. Notice the tracks are going in all directions at first glance, but a closer look will indicate the tracks have deer fawn tracks mixed in with the larger ones.

Fawns make a mess out of tracks as they run in circles, jump around and, at a glance, seem to be traveling in all directions. This confuses most hunters. Be sure to look and analyze tracks correctly so as not to be fooled. Finding only large tracks with no fawn tracks mixed in and moving only two directions will indicate that this is buck movement.

If you study small pockets where mule deer live, you will find separations in territory between bucks and does.

Ponderosa timber has to be the most difficult timber terrains to hunt. The ground is so open you will have trouble

Photo 7D

getting even a glimpse of a mule deer unless you use stands. You will need to hide either up high in the trees, or down close to the base of one of the bigger trees. There is only one place we think is harder to hunt mule deer and that is sagebrush.

Sagebrush terrain lends itself to mostly open areas making it the hardest place to hunt of them all. Hunting these areas should be taken up only by the hardiest of hunters. A most productive method of hunting sagebrush bucks is to either glass from the highest ground and then try to stalk the deer you have spotted, or hunt gullies and canyons leading to and from their watering and feeding areas.

If you decide to try stalking, you must first decide which way the wind is coming from and the direction of the deer's movement. Either way, attempt to ambush him before he decides to bed or watch and wait until he beds. Then, after he is sleeping soundly, try to move in on him for a shot. Other than these methods, we know of no other way to harvest deer on a regular basis in sagebrush or ponderosa country.

A mixture of evergreen, lodgepole pine, sugar pine and ponderosa together in one location is an excellent choice of mule deer terrain. In this area you will have many choices of methods in which you can harvest a deer depending on how you choose to hunt.

Photo 7E

Hopefully, you will have scouted your hunting areas before the season. Try to pick a place where all or most of the different kinds of terrain blend together. Try to set up your location so the deer are in the more open areas and you have the cover to your advantage. Remember, the deer is trying to have this situation reversed. Using your knowledge to be in the right place at the right time will increase your chances of seeing deer. Pick your terrain carefully and you will be 50% of the way to harvesting a deer.

D. FOOD FOR MULE DEER

Mule deer eat a wide variety of browse, including bitterbrush. This bush grows in the lower elevations. It does not grow from about one-fourth of the way up most mountains we hunt. The bush is greenish in color and if you look at it closely, it has little pink buds that do not blossom fully. If you use your hand to cup and gently pull, the buds will fall off just as they do when the deer are feeding on them. This is one of the mainstays of food for mule deer. As you scout the area looking at this bitterbrush, you should be able to see the ones that the deer are feeding on the most. They will be the ones that have been stripped of the buds. Only deer do this to the bush so there will be no question in your mind as to what you are looking at.

Another plant to observe is the green-leafed manzanita. This bush looks and grows much like a wild rhododendrun (rhodie). The leaves are not as large as the rhodie and they are a little waxy in comparison. The manzanita grows from about one-fourth of the way up the mountains and higher, almost to the top in the places we hunt. The bush only blooms about every seven years or so, depending on the elevation. This is what determines when it blooms. The pungent odor is so strong that it is difficult to breathe. You will not see bitterbrush and green-leafed manzanita growing on the same part of the mountain because of the elevation differences needed by each of these plants.

Mule deer will eat a minimum of manzanita and only the most recent new growth. It appears to us the deer do not like the waxiness of this plant. We have seen them eat some of the blossoms and lick the nectar out of them, but mule deer love to lay in the manzanita because at the base of the bush it is usually cooler and the deer crawl up to the big bush to escape the midday heat.

Mule deer savor mushrooms — white, brown or black. They will, however, eat only the top center of the mushroom, leaving the outer edges and the stem intact. As you are scouting, look for mushrooms with a bite taken out of the top. You can bet mule deer have been feeding there. Mule deer also feed on a small amount of grass, but there is no way to tell by looking at grass if deer are actively feeding. Chokecherry is another food source. However, this bush is not in abundance and would not serve well in determining the presence of mule deer in the area.

In the lowlands, (flats we call them) indications that mule deer are present are usually seen in the willows. This bush grows only in areas that have a good amount of water. Willows have yellowish leaves that the deer relish when shoots are young and tender. As you are looking over a willow patch for deer feeding indications, look for willows that have their leaves stripped to the height of about five feet or so. No other animal will do this to a willow. Combine this observation with large amounts of deer tracks around this bush and you have found a prime night feeding area for the deer in your local area.

Mule deer also feed on young tender aspen. However, aspen is not prevalent in our area. It may be in your area so look for it the next time you are scouting. Deer dine on sagebrush the same as they do on bitterbrush. We have seen deer feeding on moss, too — not the green moss but the blackish kind that hangs from lodgepole pine trees. Mule deer need salt and minerals in their diet. Rock outcroppings is one place where you will find minerals. Place a stand close to these places and your chances to harvest a trophy class mule deer are enhanced. Young saplings on tree farms are also food for deer. The deer eat the tops off of them and it usually kills the young trees.

Mule deer love alfalfa, hay, clover and a few other farm type crops. Animal feed salt mixed in loose dirt will also draw deer. Mule deer will move their feeding areas according to taste conditions, safety and quantity of food concentrations in an area. In order for your party to keep up with the ever changing feeding conditions, you must be observant each and every day you are in the field. Seeing some or no traceable marks on the landscape will indicate this spot is or is not a prime spot; at least for the moment or until something changes in the quality, quantity or safety in this feeding area.

E. HOW OFTEN DO MULE DEER WATER

Our party has done a lot of research and observation on how often deer water. Deer water mostly at night, which makes this type of research very difficult. We staked out some vantage points to see when and how often the same deer came to water. After a few years of observations, here are our findings.

Bucks are the first to start down from the higher locations, but because does are usually closer to the water than the bucks, they are the first to come out into the openings. This also helps the buck feel safer. If there is danger, the doe will not remain long for fear for her young. As people see does in the meadows first, they think the does move before the bucks. That is wrong. After the night feeding, the bucks are the first to leave and start back to their bedding areas. They have the farthest to travel and the does need to let the fawns water once again before the long, hot day begins. Bucks also want to be in their beds before daylight to avoid hunters and other predators.

The bucks are content in higher elevations as the flies are less of a nuisance. The flies try to lay eggs in the bloody tissue of the antlers where they have been rubbed to remove the velvet. Our records show most bucks enter the clearings from about 9 p.m. to 10 p.m. They will usually water first, then start feeding. Remember they have to feed for 4 to 4 1/2 hours a night to fill their paunch. Around 2 a.m. or 3 a.m. they will start up the hill again.

This information tells us that if you are hunting in the morning on a mountain and you see does and fawns, you need to move up the hill at least one-fourth of the distance to the top from where you are. As bucks are ahead of the does on their way up and traveling somewhat fast, you do not have much time to get up there and get into place for the shot. As we watched the watering holes, we also noted the bucks did not show up every night. We would see a buck one night and then not again for the next few nights — then here he would be again. We patterned many deer and found if undisturbed, a mule deer buck would appear every three days to water at his favorite watering spot. If there is water within a quarter of a mile of where the deer is feeding he might water every night, but not usually if the water is any further away. Does need to water each night to continue to produce the large amounts of milk their fawns need to survive.

After opening day of rifle season, the watering pattern will change. With shooting, chasing and total distrubance of all the areas, it would, as we say, put the deer down. There were no deer seen the first night after opening day of hunting season. We wanted to find out what was going on, so back to

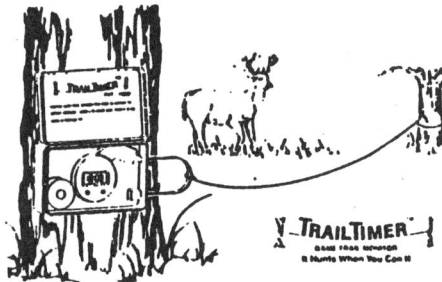

TrailTimer

Now you can pattern your game for a more successful hunt. TrailTimer monitor tells you if and when game is using special trails or scrapes. Monitor indicates date, time of day or night and direction game passes on a silenct LCD digital clock. Weather-resistant case easily attaches to tree with self-contained tie cord. Pocket-size, and is easy to use. Replaceable battery.

Illustration 7F

research. Our conclusions were that after opening day most bucks held where they were hiding and did not water. As the second day came to a close, the deer were still holding their places. Pondering this, we think we have solved some of this mystery. We do not know if we have all the pieces in the right places, but we are sure we have the right pieces.

Here is our theory. After the first day of hunting season

the bucks go into hiding. The bucks that watered on Tuesday would have watered on Friday night (the night before the season), but the bucks that watered on Wednesday did not water on Saturday night because of the disturbances. They also did not water on Sunday night. Most hunters hunt on the weekends and the pressure is most prevalent on these two days. Come Monday night, some bucks do try to water but not many. As we know people can go six days without water, similarily deer must have water, and with the days hot and their feed dry, we think deer must water every five days or they will probably dehydrate and die. If this is not clear to you, let us explain it another way.

A buck watering on Tuesday night will need to come to water on Friday night (which he does), before hunting season starts. The buck that watered on Wednesday night wants to water within three days, but on Saturday he had the HELL scared out of him. As hunters were everywhere, he decided to hide this night. His thirst increased by the fifth day, which was now Monday night. We can almost guarantee he will come to water this night or DIE.

On Monday there was less hunting pressure because the weekend hunters were gone. Our buck feels a little safer and desperately needs water. He will come to drink and you should be waiting some place to ambush him on his way back to bed. We prefer to sleep in on Monday mornings as we have seen very few deer moving on Monday mornings. But Tuesday mornings we are always hunting. This day is one of our most productive hunting days.

F. THE PACE OF MULE DEER IN THE DARK

This question was one of the most perplexing and stimulating problems we had ever elected to solve. It took two hunting and scouting seasons to complete the data and sort it all out. It all started when someone asked the question, "How far do I want to hunt away from the source of water and feed?" There is a place near one of our most productive hunting spots

-103-

that has a lot of deer moving through it, but the bucks kept their secrets of travel and time schedule a mystery from us for a long time.

We did know from the size of tracks that there were big deer moving through on a regular basis. First, we tried to sit and observe this area. That was a joke as there were so many ways to come through this area you could not see all of the areas from one spot. The bucks in this place had a sixth sense and always came through a different spot. After three weeks of scouting we decided to change our methods. We looked at the most used trails and picked three out of the nine and mounted trail timers on each trail. We had our best luck on these timers in two places where the deer were filtering into narrow ravines. (See Picture 7-F.)

A buck walks roughly 2.5 miles an hour in the dark, so if a buck has nine hours of darkness to leave his bed, travel down the mountain, feed and water, then return to his bed before daylight, and we know a deer takes 4 1/2 to 5 hours to fill his stomach, this leaves about 4 1/2 or 5 1/2 hours in which to travel this distance. So this means you should concentrate your hunting no farther than five miles from water and food. This eliminates much territory in which the bucks don't have time to get back and forth from before daylight. Taking 2 1/2 miles an hour times 4 hours travel time equals 10 miles, and because deer travel both ways, take half of that time. The deer cannot cover much over 5 miles one way. Remember the steepness of the ground will make this time change a little, but this is a good rule to base your strategy on.

G. MULE DEER STATISTICS

As we gathered statistics of mule deer units furnished by the Oregon Fish and Wildlife Department and compiled them, we had some interesting findings. First was that the best units for hunters' success was not the area hunted by most hunters. As you look at the top 5 units in Figure 7-G you can make your own choices. These statistics are based on both mule deer archery and rifle seasons taken from the Oregon Department of Fish and Wildlife biological reports.

Understanding the statistics of total hunting pressure and the length of the seasons from 1933 to 1988 we subtotaled all the information from each category. Be aware that the highest harvest success is not always the best hunting area. You must take into consideration terrain, hunting style and hunting time, and habitat availability as the key to picking the ultimate hunting spot for your party. At the end of the season

OREGON MULE DEER BOW & RIFLE 1933-1988 STATISTICS			
Areas	**Hunter % Success**	**Deer Per Sq. Mile**	**Bucks Harvested**
Beulah	38%	5.4	1,684
Heppner	29%	4.5	1,448
Paulina	31%	4.9	1,510
Silvies	33%	3.8	1,354
Upper Descutes	32%	5.2	1,632

Illustration 7G

you should see a higher harvest success ratio than you have had in the past, and it should get easier to harvest those big bucks of your dreams.

CHAPTER 8

MULE DEER SCOUTING AND HUNTING

A. CAN YOU RATTLE MULE DEER

In the early bow season, rattling is highly unproductive. When rattling mule deer, what do you think this sound tells the deer? Our observations show most mule deer will either run away, sneak away or come running. This will depend on the time of year you are rattling. Since there usually isn't any fighting taking place during most of the seasons we hunt mule deer, rattling is not recommended during the early bow season. The mule deer's breeding season takes place in November through December. Even the rifle season for mule deer is over by the second week of October.

In this early season bucks are not running with the does. The does will not allow bucks near their fawns as they sometimes will kill the small buck fawns. The does, after dropping their fawns and weaning them, will band together in small groups for security and companionship. The bucks also band together in what we call buddy groups. It is certain that the bucks do not have the desire to fight with their friends at this time. Another reason not to be fighting at this time of year is that their antlers are so soft and still growing so the bucks will not lock antlers with anything. You will not see any rubs at this time of year either.

By rifle season, which is closer to October, the antlers are hard and the mule deer will rub them to finish the antler polishing process. The does are still a month away from coming into heat so there is a lack of stimulation for the buck. But the bucks are starting to break up and run with the does. This is the best time to try rattling. We have tried rattling for bucks in August through the first week in October with no success, but it might be fun for you to try if you so desire.

B. CAN YOU CALL MULE DEER

You can call mule deer under certain conditions. In the early spring when the does have fawns, calling deer with a deer call can do two things. As you are scouting areas for the coming season, if does come running to your call you know there are deer in the area and where there are does and fawns there have to be bucks somewhere near. Using this method we have had the best success with a deer call made by Deep Timber Sounds of Oregon City, Oregon. Combining our use of this call and studying their videos, we are impressed with how well their call works.

We have tried other deer calls but always come back to this simple and complete vocalization type call. In a one week period in the 1990 hunting season the party called 12 deer, one as close as 12 feet, but were unable to harvest any. Not due to poor calling but due to poor shooting.

When trying to call, set up in a place where you have a good vantage point. Blow softly, imitating a weak fawn. If you blow too hard it will sound like a predator call. That will spook all the deer in the area. After calling three or four calls, wait about two minutes. If no results are heard or seen, blow a little harder and a bit longer. After fifteen minutes, if you still hear or see no results we suggest moving to a new location, preferably at least one mile away. Set up again and repeat the process.

In most cases, the lower elevations near fawning grounds are best for calling. The does come to the call thinking their fawn is in trouble. They are very protective of their fawns at this time of year and will come on the run. This instinct is so strong that the mule deer doe will put herself in danger in order to save her fawn. Remember the fawn will need to nurse three or four times a day so the doe will not be far from it. As the fawns grow they will need less feeding and less care. The does will venture further away but still close enough to hear any cries for help.

After locating the does, try scouting for bucks around the higher elevations. You must understand that bucks have no mothering instincts. Normally they will perceive a deer call as a danger. If blown too hard it does sound like something is caught and they will move away without hesitation. While watching mule deer bucks react to a deer call we have seen 90% of them run. The other 10% stood and listened, but none advanced any further. If they do decide to investigate the sound, they will always try to get downwind. While calling, be sure to watch the downwind side.

The most successful way we know to use a fawn distress call during the hunting season on mature mule deer bucks is not how you blow it, but the time of day you use the call. Most hunters try to use their call during the morning or evening hunts. Calling fails miserably during those times of day. Try to use your call during the time most hunters are back at camp resting, around 1 p.m. or 2 p.m. This will do two things: It will be unlikely another hunter will come to your calling and it will be unlikely to spoil your shot at a mature buck. The bucks should all be in a central location on the hill. We give you this information in "THE PACE OF MULE DEER IN THE DARK." Note how far away they can be from water. Now we all know that mule deer will seek out a shady hill to sleep on. Also in this section is given the elevation he is most likely to be at during this time of day. Do not try to approach the deer from the bottom side of the hill. Instead, you must approach him from the left or right side of the hill.

Move in quietly, and I do mean quietly. Your chance could be gone before you begin if you make any noise at this point of the game. Get within 50 to 100 yards of the bedded bucks, clear a spot to hide in, and give the woods at least 15 minutes to quiet down. Begin to blow your fawn distress call about 12 to 15 times, trying to blow softly and lengthen the calling to 5 or 6 seconds. Then be perfectly quiet for at least 5 minutes. Repeat this process for at least one or two hours. Why so long? Let us explain what should happen. If I was out in front of your bedroom window tonight and at one or two o'clock in the morning I began to blow my deer call, how long would it take before you would come outside to find out what is going on. This is what is going to happen to the mature buck that is trying to sleep somewhere within hearing distance of you. Remember, he is trying to sleep and every time you blow your deer call, you wake him. He will also lift his head up each time to get a better understanding of what you are and how far you are and if you are approaching any closer to him. Our findings show us the mature mule deer buck has three choices to his dilemma: First, he can get up and move away and find a more peaceful place to rest; second, he can try to ignore you which we feel he will not do because of the length that you will be calling; or last, the one we want him to do, is get up and try to approach this sound and find out what it is that is disturbing his sleep.

We have discovered that about 60% of the bucks will move away from your calling. About 40% of the bucks will come toward your calling, but none of the bucks we have observed will remain and tolerate your calling as they try to sleep. Another important discovery was that the 40% that did come to our calling were the large dominant bucks of the area we hunt.

You must be alert at all times or he will sneak in on you and either see you move or get close enough to smell you and at that point he has won this round.

Mule deer bucks will come in slowly to investigate the sounds when you call with a deer grunt. They will also try to get downwind of the sound so be sure to use some form of cover scent. Again, do not blow hard on the call. This sound will carry for a long way in the woods. Wait about 5 minutes between calls. Most bucks will come sneaking in so be on your toes.

Incidentally, Deep Timber Sounds also markets one of the best elk calls we have heard. It has won many elk calling contests that we've attended. The rich sounds of both calls will surely impress you when you hear them being used by a skilled caller. If you'd like to order or look at a brochure you may write to Deep Timber Sounds, 1228 Division St., Oregon City, Oregon 97045, or call (503) 656-0924.

C. STALKING OR TREE STAND HUNTING

Stalking is the most widely used method to hunt mule deer. To stalk deer you must move through the woods quietly and as slowly as possible, stopping to observe the surroundings carefully. This may prove difficult as when you are moving you are at a disadvantage. Spotting the bucks before they spot you is a must if you are to be successful in this type of hunting. Deer detect movement instantly. Deer also hear the slightest sounds and if they sound unnatural they will sneak away or hide.

After seeing something move, the buck will use his nose to identify the moving object. Most of the time that is the end of the game. Stalking works best after the deer have laid down for the day. The way to see a buck is to sit on a hillside in the early afternoon (after 11:00 a.m.) and watch for them to lay down. As you watch them, study where you may start your stalk. You will only have time for one stalk a day, so pick the location wisely. In our opinion, until the bucks bed down, you can either put on some drives or tree stand hunt. When you decide to stalk a certain buck, leave your hunting partners on the side you saw the buck. Using hand signals, such as hands over your head to indicate the buck, or whatever you have worked out ahead of time. Move to the hill that has the buck on it. Then with your binoculars locate your partners. They will indicate by hand signals how far the buck is away from you and in what direction he is.

An example of our hand signals are: Your partner holds his hands straight above his head, then lays his head on his hand, punches to the right three times and points straight down. What he is telling you is that the buck is lying down, 30 yards downhill from where you are. As you continue to watch your partner, if he points to the top of his head and makes a circling motion, this shows he wants *you* to move downhill.

At a close distance from the deer, some hunters will take their shoes off and put on a second pair of socks. They then will make their final stalk. This method is best used during the afternoon when the bucks are sleeping or resting.

Our preferred way to hunt mule deer bucks is to tree stand hunt. My son, Wes, has hunted five years and has harvested five bucks, of which two will surely make the Pope & Young Record Book. I have hunted from a tree stand since 1976. A friend of mine showed me a portable tree stand and I have been hooked ever since.

The advantage of hunting from a tree stand is that you are above the buck's plane of sight. He has not seen an outline of a figure that would signal danger to him. There is only one predator that hunts from a tree that the buck knows of and that is a mountain lion. Most mule deer look only on the ground for danger. Even if he looks at you in the tree he has probably never seen a human in a tree. Not recognizing you as danger he should continue your way. Also, your scent is higher, and usually, even with the wind blowing directly toward a buck, your scent will not reach the ground within the distance you can see in the woods.

If you see a deer from a tree stand, he is already too close to detect your scent most of the time. Another advantage is that even if you make a slight noise, with the sound coming from the tree, the buck may believe it is the tree creaking, which he has heard all his life and will not pay very much attention to. Taking sight, sound and smell away from the deer eliminates all of his defenses. This gives you a 50% or better chance of getting a close shot with a gun or bow. The tree stand can be utilized by both rifle and bow hunters. But for the archer the real advantage is that you can mark the distances each direction you will be able to shoot. By using two different colors of surveyor's tape you can mark the 20 and 30 yard distances, yellow for the 20 and red for the 30 yard distances, eliminating distance judgement for you. Incorrect distance judgement is the number one reason most archers miss their deer each year.

Complete camo is an advantage you cannot afford to go without. During rifle season most hunters do not feel comfortable in the woods in full camo. When hunting in a tree stand, the chances of someone shooting you is very unlikely. You are probably safer than you are on the ground in hunter's orange clothing.

There are many tree stands on the market today, like the ones in Figure 8-A. Most hunters have problems using the climbing tree stand. Most hunters today use a chain-on type tree stand. The cost factor puts this type of commercial stand out of range for most hunters. There is, however, an alternative to buying a tree stand. You can build your own. It is easy to make such a tree stand and many hunters do.

Acquire a piece of 4x8 plywood one inch thick. Cut the plywood into two 4x4 squares. Then cut from corner to corner to make four triangular shaped pieces. Now drill a hole in each corner 1/8 inch big and about four inches back from the edge of the corners. Cut three blocks of 2x4 four inches long. Glue and nail or screw these on the underside of the corners. Now drill through these blocks using the corner holes as a marker so you can pass cable through both the plywood and the blocks. About 20 feet of cable will do. Cut three pieces 1 1/2 feet long and place them through the three holes and attach them, using a U clamp that squeezes cable together. You will need nine U clamps. Now cut the remaining cable in three equal lengths. You will also need a handsaw such as the ones they use to cut Christmas trees, a sack of assorted nails from

4 to 6 inches and a small hand ax that can be used to drive nails and cut limbs, some 50 feet of small rope or cord, a socket to fit the nuts on the U clamps or a wrench.

The longer cable will go through the short cable on each end of the plywood, then around the tree and is secured by two squeeze clamps. Support your stand from the underside using dead poles. Cut and nail them to the stand. (In our state we cannot nail to a live tree because, in the mills, if a saw hits a nail the saw can come apart or fly and injure or kill someone.)

The tree stand needs to be at least 12 feet high or more. Do not place the stand so high as to have to shoot through the top limbs of the tree. You should be able to climb into the stand using the limbs on the tree, or screw in tree stand

Illustration 8A

climbers. Sometimes you will need to build a ladder out of dead poles. You can nail these together as they are not live trees. As you put the tree stand up you must improvise as you go. Each tree and stand situation is different. Be sure to double check everything and test your weight on the stand for sturdiness. As we will not be there to see your installation, we do not accept any responsibility for injury or fines to anyone trying to use a tree stand. You assume all responsibility for installation and use of this idea at your own risk.

After locating your spot, try to find trees that will be suitable to support you.

It is very important that you check with the state you are going to hunt in, as some states do not allow you to hunt from a tree stand. There are very few that have this law but it is better to be safe than sorry. Another point that we must discuss is that you must take your tree stands out of the tree after each season, because the plywood left out in the weather over the entire winter will come apart even if you use exterior plywood. This will make the plywood unsafe to use the next year. It is also a law in the state we hunt, and many others, that a tree stand must be removed after the hunting season is over each year.

After making sure everything is secure, clear all limbs so you can sit close to the tree. Always use a safety belt in the tree stand. We use a plastic bucket painted with green, brown or black paint to sit on. You can carry your tools and installation supplies, or when hunting you can carry your hot seat, coffee, snacks, log book, etc., in the bucket. Be sure to place your tree stand well in advance of hunting season as there will be a disturbance installing any tree stand. To prevent anyone from taking your stand, drill a large hole through one end of the stand and place a piece of chain through the hole and padlock it around the tree. We've never seen anyone in the woods carrying a set of bolt cutters, which is what they would need to get your lock off.

Never climb into your tree stand carrying a gun or bow. After you are in position, hoist your weapon up with a piece of rope, then load it and secure it someplace where it will not fall.

Using a triangular shaped tree stand allows you to change sitting direction very easily. The tree stand must be placed in the right location on the trail or it will not work as it should.

After locating where the deer are feeding and watering, move uphill toward their bedding area until you jump a deer. Mark that spot with a piece of ribbon. Sit quietly for 15 minutes and let the woods calm down. Most deer will move left or right after being jumped. After this time has passed you then continue uphill until you jump another deer. Mark that spot. Pace off the distances between these two points, move down to the lower spot and pace out 1/2 the distance of the total you had above. Down the hill below that point look for a place to install your stand. What you are doing is placing your stand just under the bedding grounds but not in the bedding grounds. Your best chance at intercepting a buck is just below his bed. You must be careful going in and out of your stand or you will disturb him and he will not bed there anymore.

Most bucks are in their beds before daylight. The buck you will get a shot at will be late getting to his bed for some reason. He may have gone to get another drink before starting up today or he may have run into something that blocked his way, such as a hunter. All bucks make mistakes sooner or later. Remember the buck that always makes it to his bed before daylight and never leaves his bed until it is dark will die of old age as you will never get the opportunity to shoot at him. The other chance you might get is just before sunset if the deer is a little anxious to get started feeding and watering early.

He will start down slowly and that is why we place the stand close to his bedding ground. During the middle of the day from 11 a.m. until 6 p.m. you may leave the stand, but be sure to return at least 1 1/2 hours before sunrise or 1 1/2 hours before sunset. Never hunt the bedding grounds during the day with drives, as this will run the deer away. You want the deer to remain there so you can ambush them as they go up and down the hill. We do make drives during the midday, but we line up to the left or right side of where our tree stands are, putting a man ahead just above the beaters. They should be about 40 yards ahead and you will need three or four beaters depending on the amount of space you are trying to cover. Be sure to stop short of your bedding ground tree stands; no closer than 50 yards is our recommendation. Making drives this way you will be planting your area with more and more bucks that you can hunt in the mornings and evenings from your stands.

Picture 8-B is a drawing showing how your tree stand

Illustration 8B

Photo 8C

Photo 8D

should be made. In picture 8-C and 8-D you can see how your stand will look in the woods. Pictures 8-E and 8-F is the view you will have using the tree stand. Picture 8-G shows the same area as in 8-F, but from ground level. The tree stand is directly above where this picture was taken and you can see how much better your view is from a tree stand. All tree stands will state that the manufacturer will not accept liability or responsibility for the use of it. We need to stress that any tree stands or ideas you use, you do so at your own risk. The tree stand is the lazy man's way to hunt mule deer as you can drink coffee and eat donuts until something comes along.

D. CAMOUFLAGE AND SCENTS

Camouflage is a necessity but most deer hunters forget about their hands and face. Using camo paint is fine if you don't mind the cleanup. We prefer to use a headnet and lightweight camo gloves. We like these because when we are

Photo 8E

Photo 8F

done hunting all we have to do is pull them off and we're ready to go to camp.

Remember, the deer will see your face and hands as you try to shoot him. Your face and hands will show up even in the darkest shadows. Try looking at one of your hunting partners in the field and you will see exactly what we are telling you.

Scents are a big problem for most hunters. There are two kinds of scents: attracting scents and cover scents. If used incorrectly they can do much harm. Cover scents should do one thing, and that is to cover your odor. Some people use skunk or fox urine and others use mule deer urine. What does a deer think when he smells a skunk? Why would a skunk spray? We believe he thinks "something is wrong." He then is on his guard and will be cautious, especially about anything coming from that direction.

As for the fox urine, we feel that deer cannot distinguish the difference between it and coyote urine, and we

Photo 8G

all know how a deer will react to coyotes. We avoid both of these popular scents. Mule deer urine is best as a masking scent.

On our shoes we use earth scent, pine scent, cedar scent or sage scent — depending on where we are hunting and which is the most natural for that area. But the earth scent will work perfectly under any conditions. We have seen numerous deer stopping to examine a human scent trail. Most deer will move away after he has detected and identified the smell.

Always use a scent vent. Never put scent on your clothes as when it mixes with human odor and body sweat it can make you break out and do strange things to the smell it produces.

Put earth scent on the soles of your shoes only. When using attracting scents you never want to put any on you, as this scent is used to bring a deer to a location so as to give you a standing broadside shot in the open. Such scents are buck lure, doe in heat, or deer, elk and antelope lure made by Moccasin Joe of Gresham, Oregon. The deer, elk, and antelope lure smells like a barnyard. It is a mixture of all animals.

Place a few drops of lure scent in a bush to get the deer to stick his head in it. The deer must place some of this scent on his tongue and then tilt his head back to allow it to go into a gland in the roof of his mouth. As he does this, you should be drawing on him. Scent is the number one reason a deer knows of your presence so using any scent incorrectly is just as bad as not using any at all. This could be the reason that you don't harvest a deer. You can hide from a deer's eyes and you can blend with his ears, but you will have a hard time covering over your scent from his nose.

We have tried other scents, but in our opinion, Moccasin Joe Ambush products are the purist and the best scents we have used. If you want more information about this product, write: Moccasin Joe, P.O. Box 1207, Gresham, Oregon 97030.

E. WASHING CAMOUFLAGE AND KEEPING CLEAN

Keeping clean and free from human odor is a must while hunting. Using cover shield products is not the complete answer. You must stop odor where it begins. Washing up every day will help some, but the only sure way to keep odor free is to take a shower. That is the only way to be sure of cleansing your body of odor.

Never use a perfumed soap as the scent in it is also just as harmful to the hunter. The deer has never smelled this before. The strange smell will give you away to any deer in the area. We use a soap marketed by Moccasin Joe. It is an alkaline based soap with no perfume added. If you are hunting for more than a weekend, you should return to town every three days in order to take a hot shower, wash your street clothes in the Laundromat, get fresh provisions and eat a good meal before returning to your hunting camp. After three days of hunting and not being able to take a shower, no amount of spot washing will make any difference.

It is best to wash camo clothes by hand as the washing machines have had perfumed fabric softeners and such that will come off onto your camo clothes. We wash camo in a pan of hot water with an old fashioned scrub board, by hand, to assure the cleanest possible camo clothes. Be sure to wash the hat, headnet, gloves, socks and underwear you will be using for hunting. It is best, if possible, to flush your clothes with water from a garden hose. The garden hose will force a large volume of water through the clothes, assuring all the soap has been removed. Then hang them out to air dry. Do not put your clothes in the dryer or you will have the same problem with the scent in the dryer as you had with the washer. After the clothes are dry, place them in a plastic bag, put a few drops of natural scents on the inside of the bag — not on the clothes. Tie a knot in the bag and your camo clothes are ready to be used. You will need two sets of camo. After using them for one day, wash them and use the other set the next day. Continue switching camo for the entire hunting trip. Coat your shoes every night with cover scent such as earth scent. This will keep them as odor free as possible.

There are various camo patterns on the market today. We prefer to use real tree, tree bark camo or plain tree bark camo. We find these camos work great under most conditions. As for army camo, we prefer to use tiger stripe as it blends in with most conditions. Our last choice is army green. It has worked fine for years but that was because there was nothing else on the market. A long sleeved T-shirt will be the only shirt you will need in the early seasons. Looking at your camo clad partners from a distance of 25 yards will enable you to choose which patterns are best for your hunting area.

F. DAILY SCHEDULES

Here is a one day time schedule you can use regardless of whether you are scouting or hunting. Rise early enough to arrive at your stand no later than 4:30 a.m. Daylight is at 5:30 a.m. during the early season and you want to be in your tree stand an hour before dawn. You will probably remain there until 11:00 or 11:30 a.m. Then you will return to camp. There you will either take a nap or just rest in camp for the afternoon. Some hunters will stalk or make drives in the afternoon. Hunting all day will be a very tiring experience.

We prefer to rest and return to the tree stand before 7:00 p.m. We remain there until just before dark, allowing enough time to return to camp. Wash your camo and yourself, set your other camo clothes out, eat dinner and enjoy camp. Knowing how much sleep you require will determine the time you should retire for the evening.

Rising the next morning and repeating this routine is what hunting is all about. That's how easy our daily schedule can be. If it is the third day of your hunt, after you return to camp, you will proceed to town where you will do your chores and take a shower. Does this sound easy to you? This may sound easy but it is a very demanding schedule. However, it should increase your harvest.

Stand Date Time Moon Wind Temp Sex Range Awareness/Activity

Notes

HUNTING LOG   Shots Taken

Illustration 8H

G. HUNTING LOGS

By using your logs from scouting you can decide where you are going to place your tree stands. You should be able to note which places have the most and biggest bucks. This is where you need to concentrate your hunting efforts. In Figure 8-H you can see a sample of our logs. It is self-explanatory. We are sure keeping logs will increase your chances of harvesting a very nice buck.

H. THEORIES

This section is devoted to our personal thoughts. Nothing in this chapter has been proven scientifically on our part.

Our first theory to explore is — do deer see color? We believe deer can see red and orange. Not as well as we see these colors but they can distinguish between them and camo patterns. We have tried orange camo patterns while scouting. The deer we observed did look at the patterns a long time and most of them moved in another direction. A few deer, after looking at the patterns for a time, went downwind. If no scent was detected, they moved but still watched that point very closely as they passed.

The second subject deals with migration. How far do deer migrate? The mule deer we hunt travel in a big circle in a full year's time. They leave the Three Sisters area soon after the deep snow arrives. They cross Highway 97 and head for China Hat — their wintering grounds. After the winter storms subside, the deer start migrating again. They pass East Lake and Paulina Lake, cross Highway 97 and go up to the high country, then across the back country towards Highway 58, then across that highway and back to the beginning. This is about a 120 mile or so trek. We believe these deer are the most migratory deer in the state.

If you want to be sure you are hunting in an area that has large mature bucks in it, try this. After the hunting season is over go back to your hunting area during the last two weeks of November or the first two weeks of December. Be sure you do this before the winter snow storms move the deer from this summer range. Use the deer grunt and rattling method. Be sure to move through all of your hunting area thoroughly. This way, you will see all the mature bucks no matter where they are now in your hunting area. You should see mature bucks with their necks swollen and full of fight. A good hunting area should have between 25 and 40 bucks depending on the size of the area. If you see this amount of bucks you are hunting in a good area and you should return there next year. But what if you do not see any or only a few bucks? We suggest you find a new hunting area for next year. Remember, if they are not here now, they were not there during hunting season.

Our third theory is — do deer have a sixth sense? We have watched deer stop at a point out of our weapon's effective range. We have made no sounds or movements. The deer have made no attempt to wind us, but the deer will not come across the opening. Maybe the deer picked out a chatter of a squirrel, but we heard none. We do not know what is going on in the deer's mind, but he senses something is not right. In our hunting area we have spots where this happens time after time. Most trophy deer have this sense and will go with that instinct.

Our last and most perplexing theory is — do deer know when you are hunting or when you are just taking a picture? Do we somehow, without our knowledge, show the deer in our body language or eye contact that we are hunting? We have had deer run for no reason. Some of the time it is when we make eye contact but most of the time the person is on the ground and some of the time we are trying to move on the deer. I tried to sneak on an old buck one time and I ran out of cover. I rose slowly, looked the other direction and walked to within shooting distance. I was able to get a shot but missed. It is very frustrating when this happens. We still aren't sure how some deer know that we are hunting them and not just looking at them but — "THAT'S HUNTING!"

CHAPTER 9

BLACKTAIL DEER HABITS AND HABITATS

A. STUDYING BLACKTAIL DEER MOVEMENT

I believe the blacktail deer is the most difficult species of deer to hunt. He is like a rebel, or as some say, the black sheep of the family. His movement patterns are not like the other deer species. How this deer can move through the thickest brush you have ever seen so quietly and effortlessly is beyond comprehension. The blacktail deer does not migrate like the mule deer. He lives mostly in the coastal ranges of the Northwest. Blacktail deer don't seem to mind being wet. The biggest blacktail deer I harvested was a 5 x 4 buck. He was taken in the Alsea unit in the coast range of Oregon in the late 1960's.

Blacktail prefer to stay in a general area most of their lives, barring any problems. These deer have no rhyme or reason to their living patterns. Blacktail feed and water at night like all deer, but there is a difference. The moon doesn't seem to make any difference in the blacktail's movement patterns. And, unlike mule deer that bed down during the morning, the blacktail seem to wander more until mid-morning.

They can also be stalked all day long if it is raining and that's what the weather is most of the time when hunting on the coast. When blacktail deer are jumped, they don't go far before they circle and stand to watch you move past them. They soon settle down and usually move a short distance in a different direction, continuing as if they weren't disturbed at all. There is so much pressure on the blacktail that it's no wonder patterning him is an almost impossible task.

Their habits can sometimes work to your advantage. By waiting a short time after jumping a buck, move either left or right and then circle to catch him looking back instead of to the side where you will be. Doing this should afford the opportunity to get at least one more look at him.

A blacktail deer does not consistently bed down before daylight. We harvested our biggest blacktail in the late morning. Even though we try to arrive at our hunting area early, it is not as critical when you hunt blacktail deer as it is when you hunt mule deer. One thing you should understand about blacktail deer is that they love to move through the thickest cover they can find. Only when the deer's antlers are in velvet is this not true. Make sure you aren't hunting in too much open terrain as you will probably not see many blacktail deer. Also, the blacktail will move across a hill on a slope more than on a straight up and down pattern. Try hunting on slopes, but hunt across them, not up and down. You will have better success seeing and approaching them if you are hunting fairly close to farmland. Also, blacktail love to stand about 15 to 30 yards inside the timber and feed for hours. Stalking just inside these areas slowly in a zig-zag narrow pattern will usually produce some kind of results.

Blacktail do not move to water like mule deer, so hunting water holes is almost useless. Yet water holes are hunted by some blacktail hunters. In the coastal areas water is everywhere and with the large amounts of rain on the coast, the deer don't even think about water. They just start feeding and are satisfied with the water content in the feed or, as they stumble upon a watering spot, they will drink.

Movement patterns to and from a certain bedding area are almost nonexistent with blacktail deer. We don't even try to find bedding areas for blacktail. The only movement the blacktail will use in any form of consistency is the movement during feeding time in feeding areas. They will normally come from a different direction each day and leave in a different direction each day. This makes the blacktail the wariest, most difficult and elusive deer of all we have ever hunted and harvested.

B. STUDYING BLACKTAIL HABITS

The blacktail deer have habits you can use to harvest them. One such habit is — blacktail love alfalfa. If you spend time around alfalfa fields you will see blacktail in the mornings and evenings.

Most blacktail do not stop to take that last look like the mule deer do. Once he starts running he will usually continue running until he is out of sight. You must see the blacktail first and get your shot off before he is alarmed and runs. The small buck in Picture 9-A is not alarmed, as his tail indicates.

We will look at a day in the life of a blacktail deer, beginning at dusk, just after dark. The blacktail deer are moving and feeding at this time. Whether they are near farmland or not, they prefer to feed in meadows more than in timber. They like to feed in old apple orchards if they are handy, or even an old garden. These are good places to set up a stand.

As daylight approaches the deer move to the edges of the timber and start to enter the thick timber. This will be from about 5:30 a.m. to as late as 7:30 a.m. Blacktail then move slowly, meandering through the timber until 11:00 a.m. or 12:00 noon (unlike mule deer that are bedded before daylight). Blacktail move around until midmorning before they begin to bed, so don't give up hunting until around noon.

Once the buck is in his bed, he must be driven out of

his hiding spot. After being driven out of it's bed, blacktail will, like all other deer, try to double back as soon as it can. It is very difficult to keep him from doing this. He is a master of slipping into a small amount of cover and sliding past hunters, undetected, only to move the other direction and bed again. But, if undisturbed, the buck will lay in his bed until around 6:00 p.m. to 7:00 p.m., after which he will begin to stir and move toward his feeding and watering grounds in the more open places, thus beginning the cycle over again.

Blacktail don't like to stay in snow-covered terrain. They will come down low, even close to where man exists in heavy numbers, to avoid having to dig through the snow for food.

When the blacktail buck's antlers are soft he will be more visible, but it seems not to alter his movement patterns much from when his antlers were hard. He is always difficult to see and he likes to move through small evergreen trees that provide him plenty of cover around his body but afford him the space he needs, but not enough to give the hunter much of an opportunity to harvest him.

Most people who hunt blacktail don't scout enough to be in the area where the big ones hang out year after year. Checking the harvested blacktail deer at the sporting goods store where I work, I have noticed, especially during the archery season, that most of the big blacktail bucks are taken in the later season. In the early bow season most of the bucks taken were small ones such as forkies and small three points.

Blacktails are vulnerable to the hunters just after a hard rain. For some reason they move on the roads rather than through the brush. A hunter should move up and down the roads, walking slowly, immediately after a hard rain has subsided. This will give you one of the best opportunities to harvest a buck in the open. Blacktails tend not to make as many mistakes in movement patterns as mule deer. This is one reason their numbers are growing more and more each year. We also prefer to hunt the evening hunts for blacktail. The blacktail tend to spend time in the edge of clearings and in the meadows just before dark.

C. TYPES OF BLACKTAIL DEER TERRAIN

The terrain that blacktail love to live in is also the most difficult to hunt. In the high coast range there are only two ways most people can hunt — straight up and straight down. Try to hunt on a slope if you can; you will see more blacktail deer this way. The ferns grow everywhere, especially on the lower sides of the roads and they are always wet. The blacktail's habitat has a large brush-like bush called, by the locals, "salal." In places it grows taller than your head. As you try to hunt through it, it seems to be holding you from going at top speed. If your arms and legs are not protected, it will scratch them severely. With the sappiness of the bush, your wounds tend to fester within minutes.

As you go through the timber of the blacktail terrain it will vary a little. There will be alder thickets that the deer will hide in and use for shelter during heavy storms. You will see patches of vine maple, some cottonwoods, fir, cedar, aspen, and some oak. These are the trees that make up most of the coast range timber. The undergrowth is a conglomeration of many different types of brush too varied to list in this book. This undergrowth is so thick in places that most hunters do not even attempt to hunt through it. They prefer to drive the roads and peer into little openings. If you hunt this way you will see much of the country but will see very few blacktail bucks. You can see in Picture 9-B, a spot from a road where the vantage point is in your favor, but you are limiting yourself to a small hunting area.

We do use the roads to move from one spot to another although, as most of the blacktail habitat is covered with logging decks. These can be very productive if you hunt them correctly. Note, we say correctly. A lot of hunters hunt the decks, but see few deer. How come! We will tell you. The most important thing you must do to hunt the decks our way is to pre-scout your area.

Photo 9A

You must know where the decks are so you can determine where to stop your rig before you drive too close to it. In the area we hunt we do not try to hunt more than five or six decks each day. This is a great way to hunt single-day hunts close to home and where you have only a small area open to you to hunt. Hunting from legal shooting time until around 1 or 2 p.m. is just about right. The first thing you must not do is drive too close to the deck. Stop well back of the deck, get out and be sure not to slam the car doors. We have found out that if you lock most doors on most rigs on the first click, even though the door is not shut all the way, no one can open your door without the key. Now move slowly towards the deck using the road. As you approach the deck, determine which side is the high side of the bank. Move into the timber and move along it until you can see the entire clearing. If no deer are seen, move into the timber a short distance. Hunting down through the timber close enough to watch the edge of the

Photo 9B

clearing, hunt in a zig-zag pattern down and around the bottom side of the clearing. Continue around and up the other side and back to the point of beginning. Do not be in a hurry as you go. Return to your rig, move to the next deck and repeat the process. Using this method will usually take between 30 and 40 minutes to hunt each deck unless the deck is a very large one.

Most of the coast range is honeycombed with roads. You might think this would make it great hunting, but there is a problem. There are too many roads and most of the road signs are gone. If you are not familiar with the area and you take off during the early morning without looking at the map and keeping track of every intersection you cross, you will spend the rest of the day trying to find your way out. If you park on a road and take off cross-country, when you come out on the next road, most of the time either way you go you will come to another intersection before you get back to your rig. At these crossroads it is going to be a guessing game which road to walk on to get back to your vehicle. If you pick the wrong way you are in for a very long walk and maybe a night's stay — outside.

Even a map of the area will not do much good without landmarks or signs. Our best advice to the beginner who wants to learn to hunt the coast range is to get a good map and go slowly, watch all the intersections you go through and maybe even put up signs or trail markers for yourself. We have hunted the coast by Vernonia, Oregon, a small town in the heart of blacktail deer country. Most of the time we hunted these places with people who seemed to know the area but several times we ended up being turned around and spending time trying to find our way out instead of hunting.

The number of road hunters hunting the coast range tends to deter our hunting party from trying to hunt this area. Even if we did make a drive and flush a buck out, we pushed the deer across a road and some road hunter would shoot him

Photo 9C

or spook him. If you are going to try to hunt these places, look for a vantage point as far from the roads as you can be, and stay put. The road hunters will also spook deer as they drive the remote skid roads during the day. The deer will try to find a place to hide and you might be at the right place at the right time.

If you decide to put on drives, make them short and quick. Hunting private land is your best bet providing you can get permission. The owner can help you pick the best spot to watch for that big buck and hopefully he might go with you.

One last word for the wise is to be prepared when you go to hunt blacktail deer. These deer will test you and your skills to the limits. The buck's cunning and the terrain that he lives in is nothing but awesome.

D. FOOD FOR BLACKTAIL DEER

Blacktail love acorns when they can find them. You will find blacktail feeding on and around places that have acorns in abundance. Blacktail will also feed on a variety of broadleafed plants. There is usually so much food the blacktail deer can eat that, most of the time, you will not even see what he has been feeding on. Normally in the late summer and fall the deer are restricted to about eight or ten plants to eat. Most feed is found in clearings such as the one in Figure 9-C. Does and small bucks, like the one on the right in the picture, will normally feed together at this time. The plants that they are likely to feed on are salal, aspen, blackberry, bitter cherry, plain grasses and shrubs. Technical plant names are unimportant to the hunter, but if you are unfamiliar with the plants we have just named you can check out a plant book from the library, familiarize yourself with these plants, and try looking for them while hunting.

Most blacktail deer do not feed on fern or pine. They will feed on willow, elderberry, blueberry, chokecherry and certain ivy. They will also eat apples and corn, and peck around abandoned gardens. All are good sources of food that the blacktail will search out.

E. HOW FAR DO BLACKTAIL DEER ROAM

The blacktail deer roam very little except during the rut. In most cases they do not migrate at all. The only blacktail that will migrate are the ones that live in the extreme upper elevations of the coast range. When the snow reaches 8 to 10 inches or so, the blacktail must begin to move down as the snow is too deep to dig through. The deer that live around farms and in the lower elevations are traditionally homebodies. It takes a very small patch of timber to support a fair amount of blacktail deer. We have personally seen small bunches of blacktail deer living in a patch of timber smaller than one acre. With water close at hand and food all around in the farmland, these deer could be easy targets if you can get permission to construct a stand in the spot where they will cross. A drive executed correctly could produce all the deer hiding in these small patches of timber.

There is another advantage in hunting blacktail over mule deer. When you choose to hunt blacktail you will get to hunt in the late weeks of November. At this time of year the rut is beginning and the bucks will then begin to roam. They will develop scrape lines similar to a whitetail scrape line, but not as predominant. If we were to hunt blacktail, this would be the time we would choose to hunt — the last three weeks of the season. Also, at this time, the snow in the hills, combined with the does in heat, will make the bucks move longer during the day. This makes a perfect situation for the hunter who is in the right place at the right time.

F. BLACKTAIL WEATHER CONDITIONS

Rain, snow and more rain are the normal weather conditions most prevalent during the blacktail season. Prior to November, there will be some fair weather now and then but after mid-November, be prepared to hunt in the nastiest weather you have ever been in. Sometimes it will rain, snow, sleet and blow so hard you will seek shelter frequently during the day.

Your vehicle must also be prepared for this type of weather. A four-wheel drive vehicle with a winch is a good choice for a rig. With the amount of roads on the coast range, there is a temptation to road hunt under these conditions. Trying to hunt this way you will probably go for a long ride. You must get out and walk to have a good chance for harvesting a blacktail buck.

During the early season when the weather is warmer and drier, hunt breezy locations in the afternoon, as the deer will seek relief from the heat and flies and their winter coats, which they are now growing, which adds to the discomfort until the cooler weather comes. If the hot weather lasts longer than two weeks, your chance of harvesting a buck will increase considerably. If these weather conditions only last four or five days, it will not be worth the amount of preparation to construct any tree stand near watering spots.

As the weather turns cold, the blacktail will require more food to keep warm. Their bodies will burn up one-fourth more energy during this time. Plants such as alfalfa, corn and even hay in the field are all good choices at this time of year. Although blacktail do not seem to feed among cattle or horses, they tend to feed in adjoining fields or between them in small openings. It has been more productive for us to hunt within one mile of a farm. The blacktail deer have become more and more domesticated as the generations have passed. Easy living has its advantages for this deer. Less energy is spent feeding, meaning more fat reserves are built up in the animal's body. Knowing this can be a great advantage for the hunter to harvest a trophy buck late in the season.

G. BLACKTAIL STATISTICS

This section is basically self-explanatory. Look over the figures shown in Figure 9-D and you will notice differences in hunters' success determined by the amount of deer per mile. We show the top five areas by putting together all our statistics from the Oregon Fish and Game Department and combining all archery and rifle seasons together. This should help you with your selection of hunting areas for the coming year.

OREGON BLACKTAIL DEER BOW & RIFLE 1933-1988 STATISTICS			
Areas	Hunter % Success	Deer Per Sq. Mile	Bucks Harvested
Alsea	33%	10.3	2,838
Melrose	30%	7.8	1,849
Rogue	31%	8.3	1,925
Santiam	28%	7.1	1,704
Willamette	39%	9.6	2,165

Illustration 9D

CHAPTER 10

BLACKTAIL HUNTING AND SCOUTING

A. CAN YOU RATTLE BLACKTAIL DEER

Yes, you can rattle blacktail deer. We know of two groups of people that have had success rattling blacktail in the last two weeks of the general blacktail bowhunting season. The archery season has a late part that starts just after the rifle season ends and runs through mid-December. Both parties were using the two-man team system. That is, one person does the rattling and the other does the shooting. When you begin to look for a spot to set up to rattle, pick a spot that gives the rattler a good vantage point. He should be able to see the shooter and all sides from where the deer will come.

The shooter should be concealed to one side or the other of the caller, but still have room to see in all directions to shoot the deer. After choosing a location and your shooter is in place, begin with a hard crack of the antlers.

The key to this type of hunting is to understand that blacktail bucks are in tune with every natural sound in their world. Most blacktail hunters that try rattling are defeated before they begin. Why, you ask? Because they do not know one important thing. They use either a plastic set of antlers they have purchased in a store or they use a matched set of real antlers to rattle with. These two types of antlers produce a sound unnatural to the blacktail buck. Here is why. The blacktail buck has heard bucks fighting before. They detect that the sounds of your clicking antlers are identical. The way to fool the smart old buck is to use a set of real antlers but use a large four point rack on one side and a small forked one on the other side. Rattling these will produce the most realistic sound you can produce and will have two distinct clicking sounds that the buck should fall for; providing he does not wind you or see you moving as you are rattling.

Then, rattle them for 15 to 25 seconds. Pause for a time to watch for the buck that will try to sneak in. The buck that comes running is no problem as he will give himself away. It is the sneaker you have to watch for. He will usually be the big buck of the area.

As you continue to rattle, make your sounds shorter and

Photo 10A

softer as time goes on. This should bring the deer in closer to investigate where the sound is coming from. If there is no response within 20 minutes, you should move about 100 yards in any direction. Then set up again.

Another trick some hunters use is to add a deer grunt to their rattling. There are several of these on the market. Using this grunt will add a realistic sound to this hunting technique. Grunting must be done in very short spurts as blacktail are not very vocal.

Remember, some blacktail will come in fast but some will come in cautiously. Some blacktail will stop short, looking for the slightest suspicious sign such as a color out of place or a slight movement as you rattle. But, if you pass the test, he will try to get downwind to check your scent. An uncommon scent will put him on alert and he will not approach closer.

We use a nod of the head, performed slowly, to indicate "keep rattling." If your shooter moves his head back and forth slowly he wants you to stop everything. These two signals will allow both of you to communicate with each other without making much movement when you are working a spot. Do not talk as this is a dead giveaway to the deer that something is not right. The buck will move off, never to be seen again that day.

The best time to rattle is in the pre-dawn and early morning hours. Bucks will normally appear out of the dark ravines and the thick cover so watch for them as they will make no sound as they approach you. An ideal place to try rattling is on a plateau overlooking places where deer tracks are present in large numbers. Picture 10-A is such a place.

Remember, you are not going to get a big blacktail buck to come out in an open place, so don't proceed setting up in a large open area. As the deer approaches, hopefully you will be above him. This will give you an advantage after shooting to see where he runs. Being concealed well and having good cover scent will make the buck come in close. It is a must to scout and have a plan before you begin to rattle. One nice advantage to rattling is the response is fast in coming or there is no action at all.

We also have added a new tool to our calling technique. It is very easy to make. It is a deadly deer decoy. Our decoy is made of two paper archery targets glued to cardboard. After cutting the deer shape out and making a small set of antlers out of plywood or foam, we paint the antlers with brown stain. Arrange your two targets at right angles off to one side from where you are and up on the highest possible vantage point so the targets can be close enough allowing for your sounds to project from that point. We also add some sticks to the leg parts going up to the body of the target. This makes your target a bit more durable. The deer decoy gives the buck something to focus on as he comes in. Without this important tool, most bucks will come in to the rattling and grunting but will not stay long. Realize, he is expecting to see the deer who is making this sound. As this is his home territory he will be determined to expel this intruder from his domain.

One big mistake most hunters make is as they see the buck coming, they rattle again. At that point the buck will stop trying to locate exactly where you are — something you do not want him to do. Now you must rattle again to get him to come. As you play this game with blacktail, you will learn to anticipate his next move. The only way to learn this is to do it as much as possible. You will definitely learn from your mistakes as you go and this is the best teacher.

As deer see their world in black and white, they have a difficult time seeing three dimensional. The cardboard silhouette is sufficient to bring the buck into shooting distance. Also deer are like geese and ducks, they do not realize size differences. As most goose hunters have discovered a goose decoy can be very large. The size does not bother the geese. To them it is just a goose. Blacktail deer look at a deer target, even though it is smaller than actual size, as a deer that is just a little farther away. Try this optical illusion next deer season and you will agree we are onto something big.

B. STALKING OR TREE STAND HUNTING

Stalking is the most difficult way to hunt blacktail deer. Even the hunter who says he doesn't like to hunt from a stand will see more deer when he is not moving. Ground blinds are adequate but are not as productive as tree stands. Tree stands should be put at game trail intersections so that the shooter can see two or three directions from his position. The outline of the hunter must be concealed as the buck comes out into the areas you are watching.

Normally, the buck will pause for a moment just before entering an opening, then pause again in the middle of an

Photo 10B

Photo 10C

opening, looking both ways for danger. The tree stand will give you an advantage in observing the bucks that might be too near for you to move without them seeing you, as in Picture 10-B. Most tree stands are worthless if they aren't put in the right spot.

Most blacktail deer hunters prefer to move every hour or so to find bucks hiding in canyons. No matter how you choose to hunt blacktail deer, you should always cover your hands and face with camo paint or a headnet. If you wear glasses, a headnet is better than using the camo paint. In Picture 10-C you will see a hunter without a headnet. The deer see his face very well. The deer will know this bright spot doesn't belong there. Even the slightest movement of a bright face will send the deer running. If you draw slowly, as shown in Picture 10-D, most of the time the blacktail buck will never see the arrow coming.

Blacktail roam the woods in no set type patterns. He sometimes is here today and gone tomorrow. Your best bet is

Photo 10D

to scout for crossing points rather than for bedding or feeding areas. These crossing points will be small, general areas where the bucks prefer to cross from one point to another, with sufficient cover to conceal their movement. These points will produce sightings of blacktail.

C. FARMLAND BLACKTAILS

Most semi-domesticated blacktail living on farmland can be hunted out of a tree stand more successfully than the blacktail that live in the thick timber. Remember, old apple orchards and old gardens are excellent places for a tree stand. Blacktail will frequent both spots as long as the apples are present and the garden has some volunteer plants growing in it.

Blacktail that live close to man tend to tolerate man sightings more than deer that live in the wild. Farm equipment can be used to scout for blacktail deer in the early seasons.

The fence rows are a place you should watch for bedded bucks. If the buck senses danger he will cross to the back side of the fence row and try to sneak away with his head down.

The first rolling hills that lead to the timber are another spot that should not be forgotten to scout and hunt. Once on farmland, the bucks will adapt quickly to the taste of the easy living. They will be reluctant to leave.

Be sure to acquire permission to hunt farmland. Be sure to clean up before you leave, even if it is not your mess. The farmer will not know it wasn't yours and the next time you want to hunt there he will probably say "NO". A mess or a gate left open and especially, a cut fence, will be the end to hunting these productive areas. This has happened to many good hunting spots, so don't let this happen to yours.

D. KEEPING WARM WHILE YOU'RE WET

Hunting blacktail deer is a wet experience most of the time. Trying to keep warm in this type of situation is difficult. Here are some ways to keep warm while hunting under these wet conditions.

One way is to wear wool. We have seen bib overalls made of wool. This will keep your body warm from the chest down even after you are wet all the way through. When purchasing socks, try to purchase the ones that go up close to the knees and are made of wool, if you can wear them. Wool irritates some people's skin, so before attempting to wear wool, try it at home for awhile. Sweaters of wool or some insulated underwear are acceptable under most conditions. Also, any clothing with a waterproof lining will also aid in comfort while you are wet. You will be wet from the waist down while hunting blacktail deer in the deep salal. Normally, you will only be wet from the knees down. We have also seen people wearing riding chaps while hunting. These are somewhat waterproof and help keep the wet brush sticking to you as you go through it.

E. SINGLE-DAY HUNTS

It is true that we prefer to hunt at least a week at a time. But not all of us, for one reason or another, have that much time. On a one-day hunt you must get to the location and set up quickly. Proper rest before this type of hunt is a must. Arriving early and planning to stay late is the key to success to single-day hunts.

Your hunt should be set in a small area. It is better to hunt the smaller areas as they can be hunted thoroughly in a short time. There is no time to scout on these short outings. All of your scouting must be done far in advance of these one-day hunts. Setting up any new tree stands, digging pit blinds at watering holes or building ground blinds should also be done far in advance of these hunts. Don't let us discourage you as there are many deer harvested on one-day hunts. If you have scouted and know where to concentrate your efforts, you stand a good chance of harvesting as big a buck as anyone else. Try to hunt within two hours of your home. This is not our recommended hunting situation as it is very hectic, but it might be just the kind of hunting you will need to fill in those one-day gaps.

F. HUNTING DIARIES

An accurate diary is the most important item on a short hunt. Hunting logs tell you what you have found out about the deer in this local area and where the most productive spots may be found. Keep your diary in a tablet on the dash of your rig. Normally you will not see the advantage of keeping an accurate diary the first year you hunt, but as you assemble more and more data you will see how it can help you pick a better place to hunt in the coming years. Sometimes it will show that if you move a short distance from where you are hunting now, you will be in a better position to size up the bucks before they come within shooting range. These little pockets are worth all the time spent to find them. These places will produce bucks year after year. Most of the time they will be crossing points or movement areas within your small hunting area. The longer you accumulate information in your diary, the more it will be worth it to you. Keep your diary up to date and you will see results in time.

G. THEORIES

Blacktails roam the woods with no real definite pattern or purpose. You will find blacktail bucks where you happen upon them. They do not migrate like mule deer and we also believe that blacktail bucks are smarter than mule deer bucks. Not being able to prove this, let's look at the three deer species.

Whitetail will go up and down the same path each day and we do mean the same path. Mule deer will go up and down the same general area — not the same trail — day after day. The blacktail you see in an area today may never be seen again. This is why we believe the blacktail have no rhyme or reason to their movement patterns. This is what makes them so difficult to hunt.

Even though the experts say the deer cannot see color, we believe they can distinguish the difference in shades of gray that they do see. To observe this, watch a black and white television set. What you are seeing is close to what the deer sees. As you watch it, you will see that you can tell the difference in the shades of gray. Even though there is no color, you do notice these differences. This is what we base our theories on regarding this subject.

Another theory we have is that blacktail deer walk roads more than any other deer. Maybe this is because there are so many roads in the area that they inhabit or maybe they like the easy movement roads allow.

We have also noticed that you will not see very large groups of blacktail bucks at one time in the coast range. We have noticed large groups of mule deer while hunting. Most of the time blacktail bucks will either be alone or only with one or two others. This might be due to the severity of the terrain where they live or the blacktail bucks are not as social a creature as some people may believe.

During the scouting of mule deer we have seen differences in ages of deer running together, such as seeing a four point running with a forky. We do not see blacktail bucks in this type of mixed age groups running together. Most of the time, if you see one forky, the other one will also be a forky, or at the most he will be a three point. Most all large blacktail bucks are by themselves.

Wes displays several antler sets from a recent hunt.

CHAPTER 11

GENERAL DEER KNOWLEDGE

A. HOW LONG CAN DEER REMEMBER

We have noticed that both mule deer and blacktail can remember more than people give them credit for. The size of the deer's brain is a little larger than a large size dog's brain. As you know, a dog can remember much. That is why we think a deer can remember more.

If he has survived three or four years, the deer has a wealth of information to use. He can recall all of the experiences that have happened to him in those years as fast as your dog can. We believe that if he had a buck with him last year or the year before, and there was a loud bang and his buddy was gone, whenever he hears a loud bang, he will move away fast. Seeing hunters in the woods will alarm him. He is used to seeing people down by the lake fishing or in a car driving on the road, but seeing them any other place in the woods will normally spook him.

All deer can learn tricks. They can learn to crawl away from danger rather than getting up and running. We have seen this happen on a few occasions. Understanding the memory of a deer is something you should take into consideration before attempting to hunt them. Not understanding the memory of a deer is one of the most common mistakes made by hunters. Deer, like all other animals, are not conscious of thought as we are, but they do think and reason things out in a primitive sense. Enlighten yourself on how smart a deer is. Watch your dog and see how he solves problems. Apply this to your deer hunting and you will be able to sense what a deer is thinking.

Remember this, there are two kinds of deer to hunt — the smart ones and the dumb ones. We have been harvesting a large amount of deer just after World War II. Have we been harvesting the smart ones or the dumb ones? Of course, we have been harvesting the dumb ones. Who has been left to do the breeding? That's right, the smart ones. You can understand now that we have been breeding smarter and smarter deer year after year. As our deer have evolved in these last forty odd years, most hunters have been harvesting less and less deer. Yet, the Department of Fish, Wildlife can prove there are more deer now than before. As most hunters have not changed their hunting techniques since the early days, this is one of the main reasons some hunters harvest a buck year after year. These hunters hunt the same places the unsuccessful hunters do but in a different perspective. The hunter who hunts the same road year and year and has harvested deer there before now sees no more deer. He believes there are none. The deer are there but are aware of the danger on the road. This hunter must now hunt this area in a different perspective by going off the road.

B. ANTLER DEVELOPMENT

What is an antler? It is a bone! What makes an antler grow to a certain size?

A trophy class animal first must have the genetics to grow large antlers. Heredity is the first factor that creates large antlers on a particular buck. The second factor is diet. A deer must have a good amount of calcium in the diet in order to produce the massive antlers we all want to see. For any deer to grow this type of antler he must also live long enough to grow them.

Without all these factors a buck will only grow an average set of antlers. We have harvested deer in one area of our hunting territory that have a heredity flaw in the growth of their antlers. There is an unusual growth some place on the antlers. The knot that we see in these racks is present only on the bucks we have seen and harvested from this area.

The biologists of the area say there was a stag back in the generations that had this genetic flaw. We have several sets of antlers with this flaw and all of them were taken out of the same area. No other deer we have taken from any other spot have had this flaw. This shows us that a stag from the past breeding season had this gene in his biological traits. Just as some human races have blue-eyed blonds and others have the dark skin where black-eyed offspring are predominant, this stag passed this gene down and as the offspring have bred over and over, this flaw shows up more and more.

Another antler observation is that other mule deer of a certain area have a strange form of tall, straight, three-point antlers. These antlers grow straight up and are abnormally spindly looking. Photo 11-A shows abnormal antlers on two

Photo 11A

bucks we harvested.

The forky shows good antler mass. Given the opportunity to live, he would have been a nice trophy. Most world class trophy hunters will tell you there are only six or seven places in the Northwest that produce world class antlers. All hunters seeking this class of animal will only hunt these places.

In trophy hunters' opinions, the potential in other hunting areas for class antlers is not there. They prefer to hunt little pockets where there have already been trophy class animals taken in the past. Usually, a grandson or great-grandson of one of these large bucks will have larger antlers than his sires. Compare a human child of today with his grandfather and you can see each generation is getting larger and larger due to better food and control of disease.

Photo 11B

C. TOP STATES FOR RECORD CLASS BUCKS

There are some special states where we would feel confident in hunting mule deer and blacktail deer. Our choice for hunting record class mule deer would be the state of Colorado. We believe this state has the best breeding population of mule deer of all the other states. Our second choice is Utah because we are impressed with the size of the deer antlers we have seen that come from this state. New Mexico, Wyoming, Idaho, Montana or Arizona also have some trophy class bucks. Nevada, Oregon and California would be our last choices from our observations.

Now let's look into our choices of states for hunting blacktail deer.

We unanimously pick Oregon as the best state to find a trophy blacktail buck. As I have worked with a man most people call the "Blacktail King" and have seen the bucks he has harvested, we cannot consider hunting any other state, except California, where we do believe there is a chance that someone could harvest a trophy class blacktail. As far as any other states, we could recommend a chance to find a trophy blacktail in the state of Washington. We hope this information will aid you in you choice of states to hunt.

A nice blacktail buck heads for heavy cover.

CHAPTER 12

WHAT TO DO WHEN YOU HIT A DEER

A. HIT PLACEMENT

If you are shooting a gun at a deer and if you are a good shot you can shoot for the head or neck. You either will kill him outright or you will miss him completely. For the average shooter, the best shot is the front shoulder shot. By hitting the buck in the front shoulders you will also hit the lungs. This shot will put the deer down quickly and humanely. With the bow, however, your best choice of a shot is just behind the front shoulder as the arrow will not penetrate the shoulder bone. Most shots placed in the middle of the front shoulder will stop at the bone and with very little penetration the buck will be lost.

As the deer walks away from you at a slight angle, you will have the best shot an archer can get. The reason this shot is so deadly is that the arrow will protrude forward toward the heart. As you study Picture 12-A you can see that the front shoulder is in a place to protect the heart. As the arrow enters back by the last four ribs it will cut along the liver and the lungs and hopefully end up where the heart is. A shot at this angle will produce one of the fastest kills possible with a bow.

In Figure 12-A you can see three arrows coming from the top right side. If your shot is from the above angle you will have a bigger killing area to hit. This can be accomplished by shooting from a tree stand or by being just above your target. And, if you are more than five inches to the left or right of the target you will miss the deer completely. If you are a few inches high or low you will still hit the deer and have good shot placement. As shown in Picture 12-A, all three arrows will hit the spine and penetrate through. Lungs, liver or heart shots are all killing shots. We would rather miss a deer than make a poor hit.

We emphasize that you must be shooting a heavy weight bow over 80 pounds to attempt this kind of shot because the spine is so hard to penetrate with all the bone in it. If the shot is high you will still hit the lungs and the jugular vein running down the neck or even the neck bone itself. If the shot is a little low, it will hit the liver, lungs and possibly the heart.

One last thought is not to take a rear end shot with either a gun or a bow. Both shots will damage much prime meat, it will make a mess when you gut the animal and

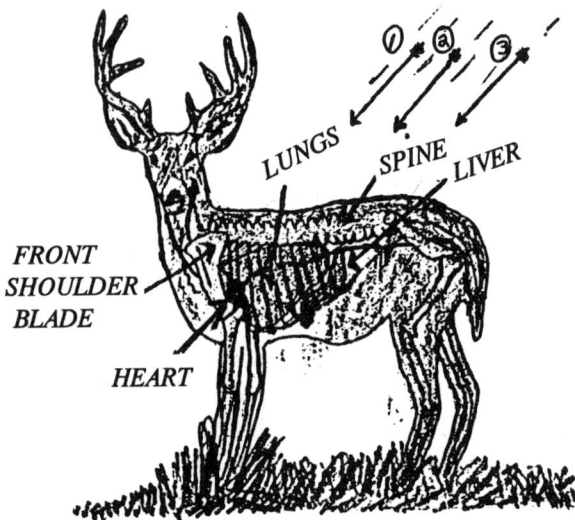

Illustration 12A

sometimes the meat will not be worth taking home. So always wait for that side shot going away.

B. WAIT TIME DIFFERENCES

The books we have read suggest the hunter wait one hour after hitting a deer. We say, if his head is up and he is moving fast the last time you see him, give him four hours before starting after him. We have not found a deer alive after waiting this amount of time.

Deer always die with their eyes open so make sure it is dead. Just touching him cannot assure you it is dead. By studying dead deer you will find that if a deer is dropped in the open on a 80 degree day in the full sun, he will not spoil past the stage of being edible for four or five hours.

The first thing you must understand is that a deer will not die in the open very often. It will seek cover after being hit and will lie down. Normally, the buck will not die right away. He might live one, two or as many as eight hours, depending on the shot.

The time span for finding your deer before he spoils does not start until he takes his last breath. Another factor to consider is, if the deer was shot in the evening, the temperatures will be cooler. This also adds to the length of time to retrieve the animal. You may come back after dark with lanterns or wait until morning. If your shot was poor and the deer was moving good the last time you saw him, we suggest you come back in the morning. A telltale sign that your deer is not going far is if his head is dropped and is bobbing or hung low and he is walking slowly. You can be very sure he is dying. But even so, give him a couple of hours. You must use your own judgement under these conditions.

Do you understand what goes through a deer's mind after he is hit? Let us explain what we think occurs. He does not know what happened to him, but after he runs a short distance he stops to see if anything is coming after him. If he sees you he thinks, "a predator is after me." He will do something to lose you, like doubling back on you or going through a rock bluff where you cannot follow him and we guarantee you will lose him or he will lose you.

If the deer sees nothing after being shot he will move a short distance and he will lie down, thinking he might feel better in time. As he lies there he becomes weaker and weaker. If left alone he will die there, but after he has laid down, if you come along and are getting closer and closer because you are following his blood trail, he will jump up and now he knows something is after him. He will never lie down again. He will run until he drops and that can be for a long way. With the adrenalin flowing he will not be very good eating either.

Most people we have talked to who have lost a deer did not give the deer enough time after he was shot to die or to become stoved up. Hopefully this insight will help you make the correct choice after you hit your next deer.

C. GETTING HELP

After you hit the deer and he moves off, flag the spot with some ribbon where you last saw him. Wait there and listen for any sounds of the wounded deer. After a short time move out of the area without making any noise. Mark the trail so you can find your way back. Returning to camp will allow two things to happen — time for the deer to lie down and give you time to assemble your tracking party.

Hopefully, enough time has gone by and your party can return to the spot. Enough time should have passed that you can begin to track the buck. In this regard, after you have found him you will have enough people to pack him out and back to camp. Doing this each time will increase your chances by 50% to recover each deer you hit, besides having someone there to take your picture to prove to your buddies that you harvested your deer that year.

D. FOLLOWING BLOOD TRAILS

Following a blood trail does take some practice. Unless the wounded deer is spraying blood as he runs, you will need some knowledge on how to properly follow a blood trail. After flagging the blood trail, do not walk in the trail — walk alongside it. Flag every ten feet or so, each time you find blood. Go slowly. If darkness comes, the blood trail will show up well with a lantern. If the blood trail runs out, it usually means the deer is bleeding internally. This makes tracking twice as difficult. Also, be sure to look on the backside of leaves for blood spots.

If the blood cannot be found, start from the last spot of blood. One person should start working out in a fanning motion. Every time a drop of blood is found, have one person stay at that spot and the other person move forward from the spot in a fanning motion. Keep working this way until you find the deer. DO NOT GIVE UP! Keep working with the blood trail or tracks. The deer is out there somewhere and you will find him.

Another aid in blood trailing is to look for different appearances in the types of blood. By doing so, you will be able to tell what kind of hit was made. For example, if there is any foam in the blood, it is a lung shot. This is a fatal shot. If the blood is dark red, almost black, it is a liver shot — another killing hit. When you see pink chunks of tissue mixed among the blood, it shows a collapsed lung in the deer. He will not go far.

Then there are the bad signs. If you see light colored blood it indicates a flesh wound. He could recover and you will have a long track ahead of you. A very bad sign is green slime in the blood. This indicates a gut shot. Give this deer twelve hours before attempting a recover. These deer usually live the night or longer with this type of hit. Do not be in a hurry to track him.

Another way to tell where a deer is hit is to watch him just as he is hit. If he jumps, he is hit high on his body. When he humps up, you've made a gut shot. Or maybe he does nothing which means you could have either missed him or you could have made a clean lung shot that didn't hit any bones. When this happens the deer has not felt a thing — just like when you cut yourself with a razor blade.

After the deer moves off, try to find your arrow. If there is no blood and the arrow isn't wet, you have missed, so try, try again. If you see the deer fall over on his side, you have made a front shoulder shot. If his back end goes down, but the deer is still trying to move on his two front legs, you have made a spine shot, or a hindquarters hit. But when he goes straight down, you have either a neck, head or spine hit.

By using the information from this section, we are sure you will make the right choice of action to give you the best chance of recovering all the animals you hit in the future. All these indications must be analyzed after each shot and applied on an individual basis. But we are sure you will be a better tracker with this information. I know you will not be disappointed if you follow these suggestions.

CHAPTER 13

DEER SKINNING AND MEAT CARE

A. SKIN OR NOT TO SKIN

Most hunters skin their deer and we believe it is the best way to care for the deer under most conditions. The hide should be removed as soon as possible, especially during the early bow season. This allows the meat to cool quickly. Use a deer bag to protect the meat from blowflies and dirt.

The wild or hot taste you have experienced in some meat is the result of not cooling the meat fast enough or in an improper way. In our experiences with deer meat care, we seldom have had any bad tasting meat. Proper care of the meat is the reason for this. Here is how we take care of our meat in the field.

To begin, we hang the deer by the head. It is easier to bone a deer if it is hung that way.

If you are going to mount the deer head, cape the head and neck down to the front shoulders or per the taxidermist's instructions. If you are not mounting the head, start skinning by cutting around the neck just under the jaw of the deer at about three or four inches. Split the hide down the front of the neck until you reach the bottom of the brisket where the paunch was opened up during the gutting procedure. Now cut around the front legs, just at the foreleg joint. Then, split down the inside of each front leg. Peel the hide from the neck, then work the hide off around the front shoulders. As you cut and pull the hide down, work around to the back side. Continue to work the hide down evenly until you get to the hips. Now go to the front of the carcass, cut around the knees and split the hide on the inside to the pelvis. Peel the hide all the way down and end up at the tail. Cut the tail off and the job is done.

Most people know how to field dress a deer, but we do our deer differently. We do what hunters call "hog dressing" a deer. This means we remove only the lower guts, leaving the liver, lungs and heart inside the carcass. After we get the deer to the hanging pole we skin him the way we described above. We bone the deer immediately after skinning him, but if you are going to wait for some time, remove the upper innards and then place the deer in a deer bag until you are ready to bone it.

B. MEAT COOLING AND BONING MEAT

Whether you give the meat time to cool or begin just after skinning it, you should start to bone it. We do this in order to pack it out or store it in ice boxes and sometimes we leave it in a cooler back in town. For all these reasons, we recommend boning deer.

Boning is fairly easy. Start with the deer hanging. Come down to where the neck and shoulders intersect. Lift the shoulder and cut, the shoulder will come off from the ribs without having to saw or chop anything. Place the shoulder on a cutting board and feel the bone that runs down the middle of it. Cut on each side of this bone and remove the meat from the front side of it. Slice the meat from the back side and from the lower part of the leg. This lower meat is good meat to grind to make deer burger.

After the shoulders are done, place the meat in small plastic bags and place them on ice or tie a knot in the bag and place it in a creek or lake, if nearby. A gunny sack will protect the meat from crawfish and other critters.

Now go to the back of the carcass and insert your knife on either side of the spine, just under where the neck and the spine come together. Cut along the spine, peel and pull the meat from the back. Be sure to get all the meat from this part as you work the meat down. If you aren't, you are not cutting close enough to the spine. The spine is a gristle-looking white cord with a small pointed bone in the middle of the top of the carcass which runs all the way down the back of the animal. This piece of meat is called the "backstrap." At the halfway point, cut the meat so that it will be easier to handle. Stop at the bottom where the hams attach to the spine. After removing each side, place it in a plastic bag. The meat from this part will be all meat with a white looking cover on one side, which will be removed later.

We will discuss more about this in the butchering process. Remember, if you are using an ice box be sure to place ice between each bag of meat to aid in cooling. A medium-sized ice box will hold one deer with the correct amount of ice in it. A too large ice box will make it hard, if not impossible, to move. It is better to have the deer in two ice boxes than in one that you cannot handle.

Now reach up inside the body cavity and retrieve the loins that are on the inside, up by the spine, then the liver and the heart. The loins are two pieces of meat that hang from the backbone just above where the hams attach to the backbone. We will discuss it later. Take a saw, ax or meat cleaver and remove the two hams from the carcass. Be sure to place a piece of plastic under the hams to keep them from falling in the dirt.

Split the hams apart so as to have two legs. Starting at the middle of the leg on the inside, split the meat to expose the bone. Continue to peel the meat until you have all the meat off the bone. Then, remove all the meat from the lower leg. This will be used for grind to make more deer burger. As you look at the meat you will see that each piece is encased in its own skin. We will separate this later, after the meat is home.

Return to the carcass and remove the ribs and place them in water to be washed. After washing them, you can cut them into four equal pieces. They can be cooked on the fire or barbecued.

Now remove the skeleton from the neck and head, cutting the neck off of the head. You may cut the meat off of it for deer burger, or make a neck roast out of it. After completing this task, the animal is boned. Remember, if you are using ice boxes you must add ice each day and remove some water. This will keep the meat cool, even on the hottest days.

C. HOME BUTCHERING

More and more people are butchering deer themselves rather than having it done at the local butcher shop. Saving the butcher fee is one advantage you will get by doing your own butchering. This fee can be from $25.00 to $75.00 depending on who you take your deer to. The butchering process is not difficult to accomplish. The items you will need are two cutting boards, sink to wash the meat, a roll of two-inch masking tape, a felt marking pen, some one gallon plastic bags and a couple rolls of freezer paper. You will also need two large carving knives, two small boning knives and a knife sharpener. You may purchase most of these items from your local grocery store. Remember, you have no bones left on the carcass after boning so you should have no need for a saw or a meat cleaver. You should have three pots or buckets on the counter with a plastic bag in each. One will be for stew meat, one for burger or sausage grind and the last will be for throw-away meat.

To begin, remove one bag of meat from your ice box, and wash the meat. We begin with the neck. Cut away any bloody meat, dirt or gristle. Then trim off all the visible fat and place the neck in a plastic bag. Squeeze out as much air as you can and tie a knot in it. Now wrap the neck in butcher paper. By using the bag, you shouldn't need to wrap the meat twice in butcher paper. Tape the paper closed and write on it the date butchered, what kind of meat and the cut of meat. On this one we would write deer neck roast and the date.

Now we'll start on another piece of meat. We prefer to cut all larger pieces of meat into steaks. To do this, peel the the outer thin casing off the meat, trim off any white tissue and tendons. This will remove any wild taste and make the meat tender. You will lose a small amount of meat as you trim the gristle and fat. We would rather have 100% of good eating meat than 125% of bad tasting meat. You can always cut steaks into stew meat if you desire. These three basic cuts of meat — steaks, stew meat and grind are the three best meat cuts for the home butcher.

There will be a long skin of tissue attached to the backside of the backstrap. Using a filleting knife, you can remove this tissue and then you cut the backstraps into roasts, or cut them into steaks. We cut steaks with the grain. Most butchers say this is not correct but we do this all the time and the steaks are always fine.

As some of the meat will remain in the freezer until next year, you can prevent freezer burn by placing the meat in plastic bags before you wrap them in freezer paper.

We plan our deer meat consumption after each hunting season. This is easy to do. If you have 52 packages of meat, you can eat one package a week or so, depending on the amount of meat you have. Try to proportion the meat to how many people you normally have at home. This way you will only have to open one package at a time for each meal.

As you trim the meat, any piece of meat that will make a one inch by one inch piece of pure red meat should be used for stew meat. Any meat smaller than this dries out as it cooks in stew. Any meat that has gristle in it or is smaller than the one inch rule should be made into deer burger or sausage. After butchering all the meat, you can start to package the stew meat. You can divide the stew meat into any size packages you desire. We prefer large amounts of stew meat in our stew so we package our stew meat in two pound packages.

This whole process will take two people two or three hours per deer. Allow more time for your first time attempt. You will become faster as you do more deer. We do take our grind meat to the butcher but we package the burger ourselves.

The advantage of home butchering is that you can proportion the meat for your family size and you are sure of getting your own meat, and all of it, in your freezer. It is truly not as difficult as some butchers would want you to think. Next year try doing it yourself. It's fun and you will enjoy the meat more.

D. HEAD AND CAPE CARE

Even though there are many books regarding this subject, we would like to go over a few items with you. If you do feel you need more information than we give you in this chapter, please refer to more thorough books. We do not try to cape our deer heads while we are hunting. If you are going to keep the cape for a mount, salt the cape inside with rock salt. If you have none, table salt will work. Cover the inside of the cape with a good amount of salt. Roll the cape up and secure it with some twine. Then pour salt into the eyes, mouth, and ears. If you have a burlap sack, place the head and cape in it. If blow flies, bees, ticks, or other pests are a problem you should pour black pepper on the deer head and the outside of the bag. This will keep most of these pests away.

Do try to get the head and cape to a taxidermist as soon as you can. If the deer's antlers are still in velvet, you must take care not to damage them in transit, as once the velvet has come loose it will hang or fall off. The taxidermist, if told, can save the velvet by a process he has available. They will either wrap them with strips of cloth soaked in formaldehyde, or freeze dry them. There is an extra charge for this service, but it is worth it to see your buck the way you saw him at that moment before it was over.

E. FIELD DRESSING DEER

After your deer is down, you will need to field dress him. This can be done in five simple steps. First try to place the deer's head end on the uphill side. Then insert your knife in the center of the paunch. Open it just enough to insert two fingers in the hole, open the wall from the center of the ribs to the middle of the hindquarters.

With your hands, roll the gut pile out and cut the intestine loose from the inner wall. There is a liner between the lungs and the stomach. Pierce this and cut it away. Reach up as far as you can in the chest cavity and detach the lungs from the windpipe, pulling from the front part back. The lungs, liver, heart and part of the windpipe will come out altogether.

The last thing to do is to remove the testicles and split the hams, then remove the anus and the deer is field dressed. Drag the deer to the meat pole, hang him and remove the hide as soon as possible. If you would like to keep the liver and heart, remove them from the gut pile and place them in salt water as soon as possible.

Photo 14A

CHAPTER 14

ANTLER MOUNTING AT HOME

A. PRESERVING VELVET ON ANTLERS

As we have several heads already mounted, we prefer to only mount the antlers of the small deer we harvest. Most antler mounting will run you around $100.00 each or more. We've come up with a way you can mount them for around $10.00 to $15.00. In photo 14-A you can see a three point buck I processed using the home antler mounting method. Saw the skull behind the antlers and just above the eyes, leaving the antlers attached to the skull plate. Peel the velvet from the antlers and stain them with oak stain. If you want to save the velvet, you need to get some formaldehyde from a local drug store. You will need to tell the druggist what you are using the formaldehyde for or he will not sell it to you.

Cut a T-shirt into strips two inches wide and as long as possible. Mix the formaldehyde with water, half and half. Soak the rags in the solution and wrap the antlers in it. Leave the rags on the antlers until they are dry. This will take about two days or so. As the velvet absorbs the solution, the velvet will become like a sponge. Then, just let them dry for one day.

After this, you will need to peel the hide from the skull. Then acquire a large pot and fill it with water. Bring the water to a boil on a white gas stove, outdoors. Be sure to boil the skull outside, as this process will smell a little. As the water is boiling, place the skull in the water but do not let the antlers drop in the water. Just the skull should be allowed into the boiling water. After five minutes, remove the skull and let it cool. If the antlers are dry, you may go to the next process, which is cutting plaques.

B. CUTTING PLAQUES

Plaques can be cut in any shape you want. Fold a piece of paper in half and experiment with different shapes until you find one you like. Then purchase a piece of hardwood such as oak or walnut. Cut this shape out and run a router around the edges. Now either stain or varnish it and let it dry overnight. Take a lid from a large plastic butter container, cut the center out of it, leaving the lip. Nail this to an old board, pull it slightly to make it pointed at the bottom. Nail the antlers to the board with a small nail; do not nail them too solid.

Mix plaster of paris as per instructions. Pour it over the skull. As it begins to harden, shape it with your fingers, but keep your fingers moist. The shape should look like a heart and it should be thin at the edges and thick in the middle. After the plaster is hardened overnight, shape it with sandpaper or a wood rasp. Shape it perfectly before you finish this step. Then cover the skull part with any type material you prefer, such as velvet or deer hide. Do not leave any wrinkles on the cover. Sew the back ends together as best you can. Neatness is important at this stage. Drill two holes in the plaque and attach the antlers with two large screws from the back. The antlers are ready to hang and admire.

We truly hope this book will aid you in your quest for hunting and harvesting many trophy deer. Gook luck and may your hunts be safe and enjoyable to you and everyone you are with.

If you would like to drop us a line about our book, please do! KH Productions, P.O. Box 634, Boring, Oregon 97009.